RARE
BOOK
COLLECTIONS

Some Theoretical and Practical Suggestions
for Use by Librarians and Students

edited by H. Richard Archer

ACRL Monograph Number 27

American Library Association
Chicago

ASSOCIATION OF COLLEGE AND
RESEARCH LIBRARIES MONOGRAPHS

Editor William V. Jackson
University of Wisconsin

Editorial Board Donald Coney
University of California Libraries (Berkeley)

Leslie W. Dunlap
State University of Iowa Libraries

Eileen Thornton
Oberlin College Library

Stanley L. West
University of Florida Libraries

International Standard Book Number 0-8389-3066-2 (1965)

The Library of Congress card number for the
ACRL Monograph Series is 52-4228. The card
number of this title is 65-19754.

Printed in the United States of America

Fourth Printing, July 1970

Preface

The purpose of the compilation and publication of the following contributions concerning rare book collections by some of the leading rare book curators of today is fourfold: to stimulate intelligent thinking about the many problems which curators and administrators are facing at a time when collections are expanding at an amazing rate and the demand for trained personnel to handle the materials has not been satisfied; to present information which will help correct certain unfortunate situations which have been in existence for at least a score of years; to establish some means for the prevention of careless practices; and to dispel the misconception on the part of many librarians (as well as on the part of the general public) that all rare books "deserve the same kind of treatment."

The contributors have had long and interesting careers, representing as they do a variety of institutions where major book holdings have been maintained for at least a generation.

The responsibility for remarks and suggestions made in each section is entirely that of the individual author and the editor. The editor knows full well that every question and problem in the field has not been solved for all time and that there is no "expert" who will agree with every other "expert" on certain matters. But, in an exploratory work of this nature, the experience of each curator may be of interest to others who are working in varied kinds of collections at institutions where similar problems are handled in different ways.

While this project was in the planning stage, a pertinent issue of *Library Trends* was published. Written by several authorities and edited by Howard H. Peckham of the Clements Library, it was devoted to "Rare Book Libraries and Collections." Since it treated all the various aspects of the broad subject, the original Association of College and Research Libraries committee of three contributors (Mrs. Georgia Haugh, Robert Rosenthal, and the editor) decided that the present publication need not cover the same overall ground as the excellent contributions in the special issue of *Library Trends*. Instead, the committee planned to concentrate on certain phases of the subject, especially those topics which were briefly indicated in a projected outline prepared by Colton Storm prior to the present editor's assuming his role.

The editor wishes to advise the reader (as well as any critical librarians who may feel that the subject is treated too briefly) that the present essays are suggestive not definitive. Books and articles dealing in more detail with specific procedures and recommended theories should be consulted for additional ideas and analyses. The Selected Bibliography, included as an appendix to the text, describes more than a hundred books and articles that treat of numerous topics related to this field, and these references should be consulted by neophytes and experienced bookmen alike.

Acknowledgments are due to many individuals for helpful suggestions, critical observations, and solemn disapproval. Obviously, in the interests of space, it has been impossible to mention every worthy collector, library, or dealer who has played a part in the history of this subject, but the authors are grateful to them for their contributions. It would be unchivalrous not to express my gratitude to Rosemary Murphy, who typed much of the final draft of the manuscript and whose ever alert and thoughtful questions regarding the style and content of the contributions saved the editor from making more errors than he might otherwise have committed. To my wife, Margot, for her patience at all times during the pursuit of this unusual and demanding project, the editor is deeply grateful, for the accomplishments of this task required devotion beyond what is normally associated with matrimonial vows.

It is the sincere hope of the editor and of the contributors that this endeavor will serve to stimulate, warn, and benefit anyone who has a professional interest in the subjects covered in this collection of articles. For this specialized kind of library work, surrounded as it is with so many diverse problems and such varied precepts (if not actual misconceptions), needs further study so that all librarians who become interested in rare books and special collections may benefit by the experience and teaching of others.

H. Richard Archer

Contents

INTRODUCTION 1
    H. Richard Archer, Editor
    Custodian
    Chapin Library
    Williams College
    Williamstown, Massachusetts

Chapter I THE NATURE AND IMPORTANCE
OF RARE BOOKS 4
    Marjorie Gray Wynne
    The Edwin J. Beinecke Research Librarian
    Beinecke Rare Book and Manuscript Library
    Yale University
    New Haven, Connecticut

II THE DEVELOPMENT OF RARE BOOK
COLLECTIONS IN THE UNITED STATES 11
    Edwin Wolf 2nd
    Librarian
    Library Company of Philadelphia
    Philadelphia, Pennsylvania

III ACQUISITION OF RARE MATERIALS 26
    Howard H. Peckham
    Director
    William L. Clements Library
    University of Michigan
    Ann Arbor, Michigan

IV ORGANIZATION OF A COLLECTION 35
    Roland O. Baughman
    Head of Special Collections
    Columbia University Library
    New York, New York

Chapter V PROCESSING RARE MATERIALS   51
     Georgia Haugh
     Rare Book Librarian
     William L. Clements Library
     University of Michigan
     Ann Arbor, Michigan

VI CATALOGING AND CLASSIFICATION   65
     John E. Alden
     Keeper of Rare Books
     Boston Public Library
     Boston, Massachusetts

VII CARE, MAINTENANCE, AND RESTORATION   74
     Colton Storm
     Curator
     The Ayer Collection
     The Newberry Library
     Chicago, Illinois

VIII PHYSICAL HOUSING AND EQUIPMENT   86
     Neal R. Harlow
     Dean
     Graduate School of Library Science
     Rutgers University
     New Brunswick, New Jersey

IX ACCESS, SERVICE, AND PUBLICATIONS   92
     Hannah D. French
     Research Librarian in Charge of
       Special Collections
     Wellesley College Library
     Wellesley, Massachusetts

X THE RARE BOOK LIBRARY
AND THE PUBLIC   108
     John Parker
     Curator
     James Ford Bell Collection
     University of Minnesota Library
     Minneapolis, Minnesota

APPENDIX   121
     A Statement of Recommended Library
       Policy Regarding Appraisals

A SELECTED BIBLIOGRAPHY   122

Introduction

H. RICHARD ARCHER

During the past twenty years or so the problems of caring for unusual
materials in rare book rooms and special collections in colleges, universities, and private libraries have caused increasing concern among
professional librarians and administrators. The quantities of rare
books, pamphlets, and manuscripts being added to libraries present
perplexing questions, many of which have not been dealt with to any
great extent in the published literature. As long ago as 1941, G. Flint
Purdy expressed an interest in the problems of research and conservation of library materials. His appeal stated:

> There has been too little recognition, in library schools and in
> professional journals in general, of the fact that the function and
> emphasis of the public library are not necessarily those of the uni-
> versity library, the school library, the reference library or the
> special library...In general, I believe that the conservation func-
> tion is being neglected, that the current Messianic emphasis on the
> dissemination of knowledge through books has resulted in undue
> neglect of the conservation of knowledge in books. The almost total
> lack of research in conservation is one bit of evidence of that con-
> dition. [1]

The late Dr. Pierce Butler, of the University of Chicago, pointed
out during a class conference on curatorship at the Graduate Library
School:

> Administration of the rare book room is a branch of librarian-
> ship that, so far as we know, has developed no literature. It is a
> growth rather than a thing planned. In America it has developed

---

[1] G. Flint Purdy, "Why Not Research in Rare Book Conservation?," *Library Journal*, 66:144 (Feb. 1941).

pragmatically, even blindly. Such uniformity as exists has come about by imitation more than through formal consultation or literature. [2]

Emphasis during past decades has been placed on bibliographical, historical, and administrative studies; investigations of the procedures of cataloging and classification; methods of book selection; analysis of readers' interests; and numerous other problems concerned primarily with the library as an educational instrument for the dissemination of knowledge. Most library courses in accredited library schools of today, whenever they deal with procedures and practices, tend to disregard the function of custodianship and point more directly toward service and effective administration of various techniques; consequently, the questions of handling and preservation are seldom considered. It is solely from the many experienced and qualified professionals working at their jobs in the various kinds of rare book libraries that we can learn more about the day-to-day problems and the many remedies and workable solutions that have proved to be helpful. These valuable contributions, however, seldom reach print and are usually available only through informal meetings and private gatherings, which may or may not include the very librarians who would benefit most by such an exchange of information.

The statement made by Dr. Pierce Butler has prompted some librarians to consider a means of establishing principles and stating precepts for handling special materials, including books and other library materials, that can easily be destroyed; small items that can easily be stolen or misplaced; materials of unusual or great market value that are in danger of mutilation or theft; and books and other written and printed materials which cannot circulate freely, such as pornography, autographed letters, beautiful or fragile examples of printing and hand illumination, as well as books and manuscripts which are acknowledged rarities.

The training of librarians and assistants so that they will be able to understand the necessity for special handling should be considered in most, if not all, of our graduate library schools. This is especially true today, when the graduates of many accredited library schools are being placed in positions where it is necessary for them to solve the many problems which have arisen in our rapidly expanding system of research libraries. Certainly most of our present library personnel should be aware of the problems inherent in the more specialized libraries. They should be trained so that they will recognize the importance of having well-informed and practical-minded staff members qualified to take over the duties of seeing that special materials receive proper treatment for their preservation and use.

The late Dr. Randolph G. Adams, renowned curator of the William L. Clements Library, felt (as did many others of his time) "that no

---

[2]Graduate Library School, Jan. 1943.

really worthy book should be put into the hands of the average barbarian. The librarians have made the subject easy of solution by ruining the book before it can be had by the reader."[3] To many people his statement is as valid today as it was then, although there are many reasons to be less pessimistic about the situation in recent years. A few educated bookmen and professional librarians have made an effort to improve conditions and have benefited by the errors of their predecessors and less-informed contemporaries.

Any librarian engaged in learning about the field of rare books should read and study the two articles, "Librarians as Enemies of Books," by Randolph G. Adams (referred to above), and "Rare Book Rooms in Libraries," by W. W. Bishop,[4] as well as the special issue of *Library Trends* devoted to "Rare Book Libraries and Collections," edited by Howard H. Peckham.[5] These present some wise observations and provide essential information of use to anyone not familiar with precepts and theories of such collections. Adams, like others of his time, offers no rules of thumb that will satisfy everyone or every situation, but there are many experienced curators who will agree with Archibald C. Coolidge, former Harvard librarian, who said: "Have very few rules, and break them all."[6]

Bishop indicated some of the problems when he wrote:

> The training of rare book room curators, therefore, becomes of great importance.... It is experience which is the great teacher. Broad acquaintance with the history of learning is valuable but it is generally gained by reading and study rather than by formal instruction... The true curator is probably born rather than made. We are fortunate in having developed a few in this country. And we have need for many more to succeed to the work which has been so well begun. For, depend upon it, the growth of general and university libraries is bound to produce more and more keepers of rare books.[7]

The ideas and recommendations for solutions to certain problems covered in the essays which follow are intended to aid students, as well as the less-experienced staff members in libraries, in improving the performance of their duties—whether professional or clerical—in the field of special collections.

---

[3]Randolph G. Adams, "Librarians as Enemies of Books," *Library Quarterly,* 7: 317-31 (July 1937).

[4]W. W. Bishop, "Rare Book Rooms in Libraries," *Library Quarterly,* 12:375-85 (July 1942).

[5]*Library Trends,* 5, no. 4:417-94 (April 1957).

[6]Quoted by Adams, *op. cit.,* p.325.

[7]Bishop, *op. cit.,* p.385.

Chapter I

The Nature and Importance of Rare Books

MARJORIE GRAY WYNNE

It is impossible to frame a brief, descriptive definition of a "rare book" that will be certain to include all the varieties, many of which are referred to later in this chapter. The discussion will cover books and manuscripts, of whatever kind, that are isolated from a general collection and maintained for use in a supervised area, thus assuring their availability and preservation.

These supervised areas have been variously named in the past and will probably continue to be so in the future. Some have been called treasure rooms or rare book rooms, with the unintentional but still unfortunate implication that everything therein is to be gazed upon but not touched. Others have been named for munificent donors—thus perhaps creating a slight awkwardness for future and equally munificent donors whose gifts would be obscured by the earlier name. Today the tendency seems to be toward the use of the inclusive and relatively more accurate phrase, "special collections." As the name quite properly implies, all the material within its boundaries may not be rare, but at least it deserves—and in some cases demands—a kind of special treatment that the general stack area, by its very nature, is unable to supply. In addition to rare or otherwise important printed books special collections could include manuscripts, archives, sheet music, phonograph records, cuneiform tablets, coins, prints, newspapers, maps, and even microfilms and microcards.

A rare book, then, is one that needs special handling, and if it is impossible to devise another and more satisfactory definition, it is at least possible to suggest some of the categories of printed material that might reasonably be kept in special collections. Many librarians have found it expedient to segregate all books printed before certain dates: for example, all books printed anywhere before 1550, all books printed in England or in English before 1640, all books printed in Latin America before 1750, and all books printed in North America before 1800. As the world grows older, a set of later dates may be equally defensible: for example, all books printed anywhere before 1600, all books printed in England or in English before 1700, and all books printed in North America before 1820.

The library that has the space to adopt the second set of dates early in its career will probably be saved the inconvenience of future transfers and the shock of not being able to find some of its books on the open shelves when the time comes to make the transfer. Any set of dates will cast a wide net, and what has escaped will then be admitted only after consideration of its individual or collective merit, the character of the collection, and possibly the amount of shelf space available.

The scope of this essay does not permit any attempt to describe, even generally, the first, early, and important editions of books in all subjects that deserve to be collected and housed under supervision, but innumerable bibliographies and other aids to collecting are available to guide the librarian in his selection of material important enough to buy or to transfer from the stacks. College and university librarians have the added advantage of being able to ask the advice of their faculty members and graduate students, and recommendations by these subject specialists should be solicited and encouraged.

It is obvious that books with a high market value will automatically be housed in special collections. Larger libraries may again find it convenient to adopt a rule of thumb and decide that all books that cost over two hundred dollars, or possibly one hundred dollars, be used under supervision. In checking booksellers' catalogs it is not unusual to discover books on the open shelves that are currently being offered for several hundred dollars, and these of course (depending on condition) should be considered for transfer.

The cautious librarian will seldom be guilty of publicly claiming that his library has the only copy of any particular book (unless, of course, he printed it himself). He may claim the only recorded copy, or one of three known copies, or something equally innocuous, but the moment that any book is described as unique, two more just like it are almost certain to spring out of oblivion. The world's repositories of books—including all libraries and all attics—are so numerous that it is impossible to know precisely how many copies of any particular title are in existence at any particular time.

In 1830, not a single copy of the first edition of *Pilgrim's Progress* (1678) could be located; in 1958 there were about a dozen recorded copies. Today there is only one recorded copy of Shakespeare's *Titus Andronicus* (1594), but who can say when others will be discovered? This does not mean that the careful census is to be discredited; on the contrary, it is to be used continuously, and the library that has one of a few recorded copies of any particular book will want to take the precaution of assuring its preservation.

Association copies, or books that bear evidence of having passed through the hands of famous people, are collected sometimes out of sentiment and more often out of the hope that they will illuminate some crevice of biographical or bibliographical history. If the most obvious kind of association item is the book with manuscript corrections by its author (possibly for a later edition), or the book by one author with marginal annotations by another, there are other kinds that reveal equally interesting and important facts. A dated presentation inscription may help establish the month or even the day of publication; the name of a recipient may lead to new sources of information about the donor; and the reassembling of a dozen books from an author's library may establish some pattern of influence on his own work.

The evidence of association takes many forms, from the simple bookplate and the certain signature, to the conjectured handwriting and the questionable claims of subsequent owners. The proved and the unproved, however, have a place in special collections, and once there, a provenance file is the indispensable tool for locating them.

A book's binding will frequently prove more interesting than the book itself—and much more important. Any book known to have been bound by Padeloup, Roger Payne, Edwards of Halifax, or a host of equally well-known figures in the history of bookbinding will be automatically housed in special collections, and even the questionable ones should be accumulated and listed in the binding file against the day when a visiting binding expert can perhaps give an opinion on their authenticity. In addition to the work of famous binders, there will also be books with unconventional coverings that deserve some kind of protection: the *dos-à-dos* binding, the embroidered binding, the metal or ivory binding, and so on. Even a binding in no way unusual except for its perfect state of preservation should be kept that way as long as possible; for example, an early nineteenth-century three-decker novel in boards with paper label, as clean and crisp as the day it was issued, is a permanent record of one phase of publishing and binding history.

A binding, of course, may also be a source of information about provenance as well as an example of craftsmanship. Coats of arms, crests, monograms, and even names have been tooled on covers, and as indications of former ownership these should be examined and identified whenever possible.

Every library will acquire, in one way or another, a number of books which are not necessarily scarce, or expensive, or even important, but which present unusual problems involving housing and usage. Miniature books, for example, if left to their own fate on the open shelves, are likely to fall through interstices or into someone's pocket. The size of a miniature may be arbitrarily fixed by individual libraries —anything under four inches seems like a reasonable figure—and all books under that height should be automatically shelved in special collections. Large portfolios of unbound prints, and bound volumes with large and particularly attractive color plates of birds, flowers, costumes, views, and the like, present an almost irresistible temptation to certain users. The librarian's first impulse is automatically to give them the protection of the special collections area, and in many cases they deserve it, but unless that area is unlimited, the impulse should be curbed and each folio examined for individual distinction.

Modern books that can be bought in any bookstore for a few dollars each are appearing with increasing regularity on the shelves of special collections in the larger research libraries throughout the country. It is not enough these days to be looking forever backward, to be collecting and preserving only material produced in other centuries; the obligation of the conscientious librarian is to set aside for succeeding generations the best, the most important books that are being published within the hour. The burden of immediately recognizing the best and the most important should weigh lightly on even the most timorous soul, for the virtue lies not so much in predicting correctly as in preserving the evidence for a later and more leisurely evaluation. The real problem is to decide how many contemporary books, in mint condition, with a duplicate copy for circulation, can be collected by any one library.

It has been suggested that the responsibility for collecting everything by certain authors be divided among a group of participating libraries (an operation similar to the Farmington Plan for foreign books). So far as the author can determine, this proposal has not been put into practice, and each library must continue to make its own decision as to what and how much it can collect. Although these observations apply chiefly to literature, the librarian must be equally alert to the first appearance in print of books on science, philosophy, religion, or indeed any subject that will add new chapters to human history. The Henry De Wolf Smyth report on the use of atomic energy for military purposes was first issued by the U.S. War Department on August 11, 1945; it was a plain mimeographed pamphlet, but its staggering disclosures ushered in a new age.

Limited editions have a place in special collections along with other modern books, but the self-conscious limitation note should be viewed with calm detachment instead of abject idolatry. A limited edition, with its wide margins, special illustrations, and abundant leading, is usually designed to delight the eye of one kind of collector, but it is not often the first appearance of the book or even one that contains any new evidence, either bibliographical or biographical. If the edition is limited to fifty or possibly a hundred copies, or if the title is by an author whose complete works are being collected by the library, then the book might automatically go into special collections; otherwise, each limited edition should be subjected to the same close scrutiny that is given to all other candidates for special collections.

Manuscripts and typescripts, because they are unique, should certainly be kept in special collections. Ranging from a single letter by a well-known author or a dozen boxes of the business papers of a manufacturing company, from a fourteenth-century text of Cicero to the typescript of a modern novel, each will present an individual problem in storing and administering.

The character of the book collection will obviously influence the kind of manuscripts that a library will acquire by purchase or accept as gifts. Ideally, all the manuscripts of one author should be in one library, thus saving scholars the expense and inconvenience of traveling great distances. But this ideal situation will never exist, of course, and the most that any intelligent librarian can do is to refrain from buying material that more logically belongs somewhere else. In the case of gifts, he can honestly and tactfully direct the donor's interest to another library where a particular gift would be more appropriate, more useful, and more easily cared for. Small college, public, and historical society libraries can best serve scholarship and their communities by concentrating on acquiring the manuscripts of local authors and of local interest.

Some people, in giving their manuscripts to a library, impose unreasonable restrictions on their use—they may stipulate, for example, that the manuscripts are not to be opened for fifty or a hundred years—but whatever the restrictions, the library must abide by them, once the gift has been accepted on those terms. In all other cases, the use of manuscripts should be unrestricted and unhampered, and when requests for publication seem to conflict, the librarian's records will enable him to inform scholars of work already in progress and, by putting scholars in touch with one another, bring about useful collaboration.

The pattern of private book collecting has shifted radically in the past hundred years, but man's instinct to possess, his impulse to collect books, remains more or less unchanged. The difference lies in what and how he collects. Large libraries are no longer being built with an excess of money and a dearth of discrimination; instead, the modern collector is likely to build around a central idea, to combine sentiment and logic in the accumulation of material that will be specifically useful. The impecunious collector who concentrates on books relating to the history of his favorite sport will be better pleased and better informed than the wealthy collector who buys the expensive first editions of assorted authors, the so-called high spots.

So much has been written about book collecting that it would be injudicious to try to repeat fragments of it here, and, furthermore, reading at length about their mania is one of the chief pleasures of bibliophiles. Alfred W. Pollard's article "Book-Collecting" in the eleventh edition of the *Encyclopaedia Britannica* (1910-11), John Carter's *Taste and Technique in Book-Collecting* (1948), and Wilmarth S. Lewis' *Collector's Progress* (1951) are among the most interesting and informative pieces that have been written on this subject.

Librarians should be particularly generous in giving advice and assistance to serious collectors, not in the hope or expectation that their collections may some day be given to the library, but in the less opportunistic tradition of guiding and educating. Occasionally a collection is generally known to be destined for a particular library, and in that case the librarian will work closely with the collector and obviously refrain from competing with him in the acquisition of scarce or valuable material. But in *all* cases, librarians, by their advice and sympathy, can make effective contributions to the education of book-lovers.

Libraries accumulate books—some that join a million others in the stacks and some that join perhaps a few thousand in special collections —with the single purpose of having them used. Any other objective would be pointless and profitless. The only difference between usage in the two areas should be that whereas stack books circulate, books in special collections are used within that supervised area, and even this rule should be broken on certain occasions: for example, when a lecturer asks permission to show some particularly pertinent material to his assembled students.

To try to justify the collection and preservation of rare books seems hardly necessary. Civilization has always rested simply and solely upon the transmission of ideas from century to century, and there is only one way of transmitting these ideas—by words, written originally on clay tablets, papyri, and scrolls, and eventually in manuscript codices and printed books. Many words, and thus many ideas, *have* been preserved; many others have fallen before such assorted enemies of books as fires, floods, wars, censors, and certain librarians. The ranks of all the enemies, however, are being gradually diminished, and the most obvious reason for this lies in the quickened conscience of the keepers of books, in their recognition of responsibility for providing clean, safe quarters for all kinds of records of human accomplishment.

Such records are discovered in the most diverse forms and places. A letter from Columbus, describing his discovery of America, was printed in Barcelona in 1493; it was a small and unpretentious piece for such an important announcement, and the wonder is that a single copy has managed to survive. Three hundred and fifty years later, as the new continent was expanding westward, other announcements were appearing in equally ephemeral form: in newssheets issued from changing frontiers; in maps and sketches of uncharted territory; in simple, unlettered accounts of the events of everyday life. These are the sources of history, and they are used constantly to document, to explain, and in some cases to guide and instruct.

Wholly apart from the continuity of ideas and facts, books provide the chief record of man's emotional history. Through poetry, drama, and story they offer an aesthetic experience which delights, inspires, and frequently transforms the reader. This experience may come as readily from a modern reprint as from a first edition published several hundred years ago, but such an experience would never have been possible without the preservation of at least one copy of the original edition.

Bibliography, or the systematic historical and technical study of books, depends not on the preservation of first editions alone but also on the accumulation of subsequent important editions and all their variants. Most authors and many editors have had second thoughts about their work—thoughts dictated by discretion, by new evidence, by the muses—and many of these thoughts have been incorporated into new issues or editions. In the first edition of his *Life of Samuel Johnson* (1791), Boswell included some very frank quotations from Johnson on the subject of conjugal infidelity. Belated discretion led him to cancel that page and substitute a new one, but the evidence is still to be found in a few copies with the uncanceled leaf.

When William Caxton printed Chaucer's *Canterbury Tales* for the first time about 1478, he unwittingly used for his text a manuscript that was singularly imperfect. Someone who bought a copy of the first edition pointed out the imperfections to Caxton and offered to lend him a more nearly perfect manuscript; Caxton accepted and about 1484 printed the second but more accurate edition. Until the nineteenth century, authors frequently strolled into printing offices, looked over the sheets as they came from the presses, and rewrote passages on the spot. The library that has the first five editions of Dryden's *The Conquest of Granada* standing side by side on its shelves has every edition that could have been seen and changed before the author's death in 1700. Individually they may have a modest value, but collectively they present a bibliographical phalanx that may be essential in establishing the text.

The aim of the bibliographer, the literary historian, and the critic is to get as close to the author at work as is humanly possible after a lapse of a few years or a few hundred years. The manuscript, the corrected proof, the first edition, and all subsequent editions published during the author's lifetime—these are the pieces of evidence that many librarians and book collectors are dedicated to discovering and preserving.

The ideas, the stories, the facts that are printed on their pages are, of course, the chief reason for the existence of books, but as physical objects they can please and instruct as well. The history of the publishing and printing trades can be discovered in the various forms and shapes that books have taken over the years, and much of the history of papermaking, type founding, and the tanning and tooling of leather can be traced in the systematic study of books—the only objects that combine the products of these various trades. Superior skill in designing books and their bindings has been recognized and admired from the time of Gutenberg to the present day, and the pleasure derived from examining and handling well-made books is exceeded only by the pleasure and the profit of absorbing their contents.

Chapter II

The Development of Rare Book Collections in the United States

EDWIN WOLF 2nd

The collection of rare books is never one of the earlier manifestations of a frontier society. Historically, it flourishes only in a highly developed, cultural center. Hence, it is not surprising that bibliophilism, in its esoteric sense, did not appear in the United States until a metropolitan milieu came into being, did not gain momentum until wealth and circumstances created a Medicean upper class, and did not spread throughout the country until new institutional centers of culture and their concomitant influences prepared a climate apt for so sophisticated an appreciation as that of rare books.

From the earliest colonial times until the age of Jackson, book collections were—with few exceptions—utilitarian in character, the books having been acquired subjectively for the matter contained in them, and not as rarities or objects of research. The statement of Storm and Peckham that "some individuals began collecting books, mainly because that was the only method of providing themselves with something to read" is generally valid for this period.[1] Although Cotton Mather owned a First Folio of Shakespeare, an oasis in a desert of theology, this valuable item was certainly acquired to read and not for its significance as a first edition.

The institutional and private libraries of the seventeenth and eighteenth centuries were formed by an accretion of books to be read. Among the former, Harvard (1638), William and Mary (1693), Yale (1701), Princeton (College of New Jersey) (1746), and Columbia (King's College) (1757) were the most important academic libraries. The Library Company of Philadelphia (1731), the Charleston Library Society (1748), and the New York Society Library (1754) were representative of the subscription libraries—forerunners of today's public libraries—which were to be found in scores of cities and towns along the eastern

---

[1] Colton Storm and Howard Peckham, *Invitation to Book Collecting* (New York: Bowker, 1947), p.35.

seaboard. That these libraries acquired books which are now considered rare has been due to the passage of time and the widening of the
definition of a rare book. Typical would have been the attitude of the
directors of the Library Company of Philadelphia, who ordered a halt
put to the shipment of the grubby, early-seventeenth-century quartos
dealing with the colonization of America which a farsighted Franklin
asked the Library's London agent to look for and buy. Furthermore,
all the old institutions were in the habit of discarding old and/or worn
copies of any edition when a new and/or better one came on the shelves.
Harvard conducted duplicate sales from the seventeenth century on.

Most of the private individuals who gathered large collections were
impelled by the same motives as the institutions—they wanted certain
works for reading purposes. Some of these were available only in
early editions; they were "out-of-print" and were sold as secondhand
books, not as "rare" books. Large libraries of this nature, including
many sixteenth-century books and even a few incunabula, had been
formed by the middle of the eighteenth century by the Mather family of
Boston; Governor John Winthrop, Jr., of Connecticut; William Byrd of
Virginia; Governor John Montgomerie of New York; and James Logan
and Isaac Norris, Jr., of Philadelphia. Lists survive of some hundreds
of early Latin titles bought as ordinary secondhand books by Norris
from the bookseller "B. Franklin." Of the major colonial libraries
only that of Thomas Prince of Boston can be classified as a rare book
collection in the sense that it was a specialized research collection
acquired according to plan and aiming at completeness in a chosen
field. Prince gathered together all the books and manuscripts he could
find relating to the establishment and development of Massachusetts.
His "New England Library" can be considered the earliest American
collection which in concept and content meets today's definition of a
rare book collection.

The libraries of Franklin, John Dickinson, John Adams, and Jefferson were large for their day, but, except for some thousand seventeenth-century pamphlets which Franklin bought as antiquarian curi-
osities and a number of early Americana which Jefferson specifically
sought out, their books were acquired without thought for their rarity
or value as objects. On the other hand, the Swiss-born Pierre Eugene
du Simitière, planning to write a history of America, made a small but
valuable collection of American pamphlets and broadsides, much in the
manner of the famous annalist and bibliographer Narcissus Luttrell,
recognizing their ephemeral nature and frequently noting the date and
circumstances of their acquisition.

The first collector of rare books *qua* rare books was the wealthy
merchant William Mackenzie, about whom little is known except that
he was a bibliophile and generous. Philadelphia in the 1800's was his
metropolitan milieu. He bought such items as Voragine's *Golden Leg-
end*, the first Caxton to reach America; a Jenson Pliny on vellum;
early French romances of chivalry; and rarities from the dispersed
libraries of William Byrd and Benjamin Franklin.

At the same time, a few men like the Rev. Dr. William Bentley of Salem and Judge James Winthrop of Cambridge (who inherited his scientist-father's books) were gathering libraries of more than pragmatic usefulness. Another collection of note was that of Thomas Wallcut of Boston, who, Bentley wrote in 1800, owned "the greatest collection of American books in America." His huge accumulation of pamphlets went to the American Antiquarian Society and other of his books to Bowdoin.

The end of the eighteenth century saw the beginnings of specialized collections such as those of the American Philosophical Society and the Pennsylvania Hospital. Yet more important as a trend was the establishment of the Massachusetts Historical Society in 1791, the New-York Historical Society in 1804, the American Antiquarian Society in 1812, and the Historical Society of Pennsylvania in 1824. Apparently by the early nineteenth century the country had become old enough to give serious thought to the preservation of its records, and during succeeding decades more societies were formed for this purpose. The historical societies began gathering archives of printed and manuscript materials dealing with their own regions. Isaiah Thomas, the founder of the American Antiquarian Society, went further afield and gathered newspapers and imprints from all parts of the country.

At first, this collecting was basically for archival purposes, and the idea of intrinsic value was not realized. But after many years it was recognized that these and the many later, similar collections were, in fact, specialized collections of rare books and manuscripts. In the sense that they were specialized collections, they were the first rare book libraries in the country. It should be noted that the Library of Congress, although it bought Jefferson's library in 1815 to replace its earlier destroyed collection, at first did not consider its books rare books in any sense and saw itself solely as a reference library.

By the middle of the nineteenth century there emerged a substantial number of individuals and dealers who devoted themselves to the pursuit and acquisition of rarities, as well as auction houses which regularly sold them. It has not been noted before, I believe, that the American rare book market was so vigorous that as early as 1838 the auctioneers Cooley and Bangs of New York could offer books from such great English libraries as those of the Duke of Gloucester, the Duke of Sussex, the Earl of Guilford, and Richard Heber and the more specialized continental collection of George Kloss.

Collecting along general lines were such men as John Allan of New York and Zelotes Hosmer of Boston. Another man who bought books on the international market was George Ticknor, who, as source material for his history of Spanish literature, gathered as complete a library on that subject as extensive travel in Europe and correspondence with agents and dealers, notably Obadiah Rich, permitted. His collection, which he boasted surpassed that of the British Museum in his chosen field, was the earliest American collection to have a world-wide reputation. Ticknor left it to the Boston Public Library which he helped found in 1852, thereby forming the nucleus of the earliest rare book collection to evolve in a public library.

Most of the interest of American collectors was, however, in Americana. John Carter Brown, a member of a wealthy Providence family of merchants, impressed by Bishop White Kennett's pioneering idea of collecting the printed sources of American discovery and exploration, began through the expatriate American dealers of London, Obadiah Rich and Henry Stevens of Vermont, to amass Americana up to 1700, and then, as the collection grew, to 1800. With an adequate purse and the dedication of a bibliophile, he built a superb collection of American rarities, together with some Aldines and Bibles. His son added to the collection and in 1900 gave it to Brown University.

Contemporaneously with John Carter Brown, the less wealthy Peter Force was gathering manuscripts and pamphlets dealing with all aspects of American life. He published a number of books based on his historical materials, and in 1867 the Force collection was bought by the Library of Congress, which by that time saw itself as *the* national library in the sense that the British Museum was *the* national library of Great Britain.

Competing with Brown for the great items of American interest—the rivalry spurred on by the enterprising Henry Stevens—was James Lenox of New York. His library in some respects (for instance, Americana Vetustissima) surpassed that of his Providence competitor, and he extended his interests to include the first Gutenberg Bible to come to American shores, Caxtons, Shakespeare Folios, Milton and Bunyan collections, and other choice volumes. In 1870 he established his library in trust for the use of scholars—the first American library of rare books established as an institution by an individual. In 1895 the Lenox Library was joined with other trusts to form the New York Public Library, and became the nucleus of the largest concentration of rare book collections in any American public library.

One of the advantages which the nineteenth-century collector enjoyed was the vast supply of important items on the book market. His great disadvantage was that he had few bibliographical guides; he had to pioneer. A man with imagination and energy could form a specialized collection almost without competition. Samuel G. Drake brought together two collections of books on the American Indian, and Thomas W. Field made another which formed the basis of his bibliography.[2] A collection of American poetry and plays, begun by Albert Q. Greene, was increased by C. Fiske Harris and, in 1884, given to Brown University. Hubert H. Bancroft, seeking source materials for his histories of the far-western states, amassed a huge collection which was sold in 1907 to the State of California and deposited in the University of California, at Berkeley. Lyman C. Draper bought pamphlets by the

---

[2]Thomas Warren Field, *An Essay towards an Indian Bibliography. Being a Catalogue of Books, Relating to the History,* [etc.] *of the American Indians* ... (New York: Scribner, Armstrong, and Co., 1873).

thousands, and manuscripts as well, dealing with the development of the West and gave them to the Wisconsin Historical Society.

Amateurs, too, collecting not for personal research purposes but out of the sheer joy of bibliophilism, entered the field in greater numbers as both wealth and interest in old books increased. George Brinley, who was his own book scout, bought privately and at auction, and occasionally from dealers like Stevens after the latter's wealthier clients had had the first refusal. After Brinley's death his collection was dispersed in five sales, from 1879 to 1893, and still remains the greatest collection of Americana ever sold at auction. Other collectors, like Colonel Thomas Aspinwall, Edward A. Crowninshield, William Menzies (whose Bradford imprints included many items never sold again), Samuel L. M. Barlow, and Henry C. Murphy, made extensive collections which eventually found their way back into the book market.

The last quarter of the nineteenth century marked the beginning of the golden age of collecting in America. Vast fortunes were being accumulated; taxes were insignificant; American "society" was evolving; and books as a manifestation of culture became a sign of status. It was a sign of the times that in 1884 the Grolier Club, America's first national club of book collectors, was founded. This was quickly followed in Boston by the Club of Odd Volumes (1886), in Cleveland by the Rowfant Club (1892), in Philadelphia by the Philobiblon Club (1893), in Chicago by the Caxton Club (1895), and others. The first president of the Grolier Club was Robert Hoe, who brought together the richest and most diversified collection of rare books the country, up to then, had known. Superb illuminated manuscripts vied with the rarities of Elizabethan literature, Caxtons jostled two copies of the Gutenberg Bible, Grolier bindings gleamed next to prize pieces of Americana. When the collection was sold in four sales in 1911-12, it realized the colossal total of $1,932,056.

Among those who helped to found the Grolier Club were William Loring Andrews, a collector of fine bindings, and Brayton Ives who owned choice pieces in many fields. Beverly Chew, in his day an expert on bibliographical points, soon joined them; he made collections of English and American literature. Also active at the turn of the century were Levi Z. Leiter and Robert Goelet, both buyers of Americana; Frederic R. H. Halsey, who collected prints and English literature; and William H. Arnold, J. C. Chamberlain, and Stephen H. Wakeman, all collectors of American literature. It is impossible to list all the bibliophiles of note, but mention should be made of Daniel Willard Fiske whose collections of Dante and Petrarch went to Cornell; Adolph Sutro, a pioneer collector of fifteenth-century books whose collection was partially destroyed in the San Francisco fire; John Boyd Thacher whose incunabula were given to the Library of Congress; and General Rush C. Hawkins whose extensive collections of specimens of fifteenth-century printing formed the Annmary Brown Memorial Library. Even more important was the collection of material on Spanish exploration, books and manuscripts relating to the Indians, and other Americana which Edward E. Ayer gave to the Newberry Library.

It was certainly the dealer Henry Stevens who, more than any other individual, created the aura of excitement which resulted in acquisitions of rare books by individuals and libraries. Experts, such as Henry Harrisse, Joseph Sabin, and Charles R. Hildeburn, stimulated collecting by their bibliographies. The accumulation of catalogs of important auction sales began to build up a corpus of additional reference, many of them compiled by Sabin who himself conducted the sales for the auction houses. The rare book was at last being defined, described, and set apart. Not only private collectors caught the spark from what was now more cohesively a rare book world, but libraries, too, began to look on their accumulations of the past with a new eye and to seek to increase their collections by purchase and gift.

Stevens was able to convince a group of Bostonians to buy a substantial portion of George Washington's library *en bloc* for the venerable Boston Athenaeum, which had never thought in terms of special collections. Stevens also sold the Franklin Papers he discovered in England to the Library of Congress. Old South Church was prevailed upon to transfer the custody of the neglected and pilfered Prince Library to the Boston Public Library. Nonetheless, "rare" books, categorized in each institution by the librarian's own rule of thumb, had received little extra or special care beyond their placement in a locked closet or even treasure room. This was the horrendous era of library stamps on titles, maps, and plates, and of haphazard and inexpert rebinding. The librarians of most institutions with extensive holdings of old books—and these were still chiefly the old libraries and historical societies—were historians, men like Samuel Allibone and Justin Winsor.

It is significant that the only American libraries listed by symbol in the first volume of Joseph Sabin's *A Dictionary of Books Relating to America*, 1868, were the Astor, Boston Public, Library of Congress, Harvard, Massachusetts Historical Society, New-York Historical Society, Library Company of Philadelphia, Pennsylvania State, New York State, and American Antiquarian Society, to which should be added the collections of Brown and Lenox which were later institutionalized. How little this situation had changed even when Charles Evans published the first volume of his *American Bibliography*, 1903, is apparent in the symbols to be found there—the same as in Sabin with New York Public now substituted for Astor and Lenox, the Historical Society of Pennsylvania rightly featured instead of the Pennsylvania State Library, and the Boston Athenaeum added.

The beginning of the modern period, so far as institutions were concerned, may be said to date from the appointment of Wilberforce Eames in 1893 as librarian of the Lenox Library. Eames, a prodigious worker and America's foremost bibliographer, became the unassuming, intellectual leader of the rare book world and greatly influenced the development of professional rare book librarians, as contrasted with public library or university librarians or historians. His influence was paramount in strengthening and making known the New York Public Library collections. From historical societies emerged men like Clarence S. Brigham to revitalize the American Antiquarian Society, Lawrence C. Wroth to build eminently on the strong foundations of the John Carter Brown Library, and George Parker Winship to stimulate an interest in the treasures of Harvard.

Simultaneously, book collectors of great wealth began to think more and more in terms of personal monuments, although, to be sure, there were many who continued to form great collections without any concern but the delight of collecting. J. Pierpont Morgan, a Renaissance prince in his appetite for treasures, bought whole collections as other men bought individual books. Onto his shelves came the stock of the bookseller James Toovey, the Theodore Irwin collection with its magnificent "Golden Gospels," the superb manuscripts and books of Richard Bennett with no fewer than thirty-two Caxtons, most of George B. De Forest's library, Lewis Burchard's medieval romances, the Amherst Caxtons, and, of course, individual items which he—and later his son— added with the advice of their librarian, the talented Belle da Costa Greene. In 1924 the Pierpont Morgan Library was made into a trust for the use of the public.

The flow of great books into the markets of the world, stimulated by the prosperity of the maturing industrial age, in turn stimulated collecting. William A. White of Brooklyn, with a connoisseurship still unusual in a private American collector, brought together a rich collection of Elizabethan rarities and the finest group of Blake items in private hands. Americans were beginning to broaden their scope. Charles W. Frederickson was able to boast a distinguished collection of Shelley. Marsden J. Perry amassed a library of Shakespeareana which, at the beginning of the twentieth century, had no peer in America. John Augustin Daly specialized in the theater, and Thomas J. McKee accumulated a well-selected collection of literary firsts.

In the field of Americana, Wymberley Jones De Renne made a remarkable collection of books on Georgia, which eventually was sold to the University of Georgia. Clarence M. Burton collected material on Detroit and the Middle West, which was given to the Detroit Public Library, and Governor Samuel W. Pennypacker gathered a large library strong in early Pennsylvania imprints, Frankliniana, and Pennsylvania-German items.

With the Hoe sale in 1911-12 the American rare book world demonstrated that it had reached maturity as an international center. It was the first major sale of the Anderson Galleries, which was thereafter to play a leading role in book auctions. The sale was dominated by the dealer George D. Smith, America's first entrepreneur of rare books on a large scale, and he acted as agent for Henry E. Huntington, who for fifteen years bought rare books quantitatively at a rate never seen before or after.

No longer a young man when he began collecting, Huntington felt pressed for time and bought voraciously and *en bloc*. The fine E. Dwight Church collections of English literature and Americana were his first major purchases. He swept the Hoe sales. He added quickly the choice collections of Beverly Chew and Frederic R. H. Halsey. In successive gulps he swallowed up the plays and Caxtons from the Duke of Devonshire's library, the chief portion of the Bridgewater House Library, and the Americana from the Britwell Library of W. H. Christie-Miller. At first through Smith and, after his death in 1920, through Dr. A. S. W. Rosenbach, Huntington bought so much in so many fields that his collection overnight, as it were, became preeminent in America in incunabula and early English books. The cream and bulk of the public Britwell sales, the early American imprints of Wilberforce Eames and Simon Gratz, and the Western Americana of Henry R. Wagner swelled his library. By deeds of gift in 1919-22, the library and art gallery were established in San Marino, California, as a public trust, with George Watson Cole as Mr. Huntington's first librarian.

Although the size and scope of Huntington's collecting towered above his generation, other men of wealth were amassing collections of great importance. Young Harry E. Widener, under the guidance of Rosenbach, began building a strong library of English literature with emphasis on Dickens, Cruikshank, and Stevenson. After his tragic death in 1912 in the *Titanic* disaster, his mother continued the collection, gave it to Harvard, and built the Widener Memorial Library in which it was housed. Luther S. Livingston, formerly a bookseller and bibliographer, was its first librarian and the first rare book librarian at Harvard. George Parker Winship succeeded him. Simultaneously, Joseph E. Widener began collecting books, as well as paintings, and his Gutenberg Bible eventually went to Harvard; his superb Shakespeare Folios and small but choice collection of illuminated manuscripts to the Free Library of Philadelphia; and his outstanding collection of French eighteenth-century illustrated books—rich in bindings, original drawings, and proof prints—to the National Gallery in Washington.

A new rare book center came into being when the English literature collection of John H. Wrenn of Chicago was purchased for the University of Texas in 1918. To these were added some time later the supplementary collections of George A. Aitken and Miriam L. Stark. In 1911, Alexander Smith Cochran brought Yale into the limelight by giving to the Elizabethan Club there the Huth Shakespeares which he had bought *en bloc*, together with the other choice volumes of the period. One year later, William Augustus Spencer willed his exquisite collection of fine, illustrated books in fine bindings to the New York Public Library, to which institution the scholarly Fords—Gordon Lester Ford, Paul Leicester Ford, and Worthington Chauncey Ford—earlier had presented their vast accumulation of books and pamphlets on American history and political economy. Institutions were beginning to emerge as a major factor in rare book collecting.

From the end of World War I until the depression of the 1930's,

rare books and rare book collecting benefited from the kind of glamorous publicity which had been reserved in America to baseball, the
movies, and politics. Auction sales, with Mitchell Kennerley's Anderson Galleries vying with the older American Art Association until the
two were merged by Cortlandt Field Bishop in 1929, caught headlines
with record prices. A. Edward Newton—collector, essayist, and col-
orful personality—captivated a wide public with his *Amenities of Book-
Collecting* and other volumes. And Dr. A. S. W. Rosenbach, book
salesman extraordinary, captured the imagination of collectors with
his enthusiasm and the great books he was able to offer them, and the
interest of the world with the prices he paid and the stories he told.

The prices of rare books doubled and tripled within two decades.
The book market flourished. The postwar imposition of income taxes
was soon forgotten by the wealthy. A host of dealers—Lathrop C.
Harper, Gabriel Wells, Drake, Goodspeed, Madigan, Sessler, and
others—helped to push along the boom. Some collectors sold their libraries in the lush years, and their books added fuel to the collecting
fires. Clarence S. Bement, Harry B. Smith, and James W. Ellsworth
disposed of their books to or through Rosenbach. Henry F. De Puy
sold his Indian treaties and other Americana at auction, whither also
went the English literature of Winston H. Hagen; the Elizabethan collection of Herschel V. Jones (who promptly began to collect Americana);
the great collection of the authors of the Romantic Revival formed by
H. Buxton Forman and obtained privately by John B. Stetson, Jr.; the
various books of Herman Leroy Edgar; the Victorians of George Barr
McCutcheon; and the modern first editions of John Quinn.

Among the collectors who were active at this time were a number
who planned to establish their libraries as institutions, some who decided at some point to give their books to an established library, and
others who had no plans. Henry C. Folger, buying only less lavishly
than Huntington, formed a huge collection of books relating to Shakespeare and his times, which in fact covered the whole field of early
English literature. First Folios literally by the dozen—the spoils of
London and New York auctions and of private caches—flowed to him.
In 1928, he drew up a deed of gift donating his library to Amherst College as trustees for the public; after his death, the Folger Shakespeare
Library was built to house the books, with Dr. Joseph Q. Adams as its
first director.

William L. Clements, specializing in books and manuscripts on the
American Revolution, gave his books and a building to the University of
Michigan in 1923 and provided in his will that it should be permitted to
purchase his extensive Shelburne, Clinton, Germaine, Gage, and
Greene Papers. Alfred C. Chapin, seeking high spots in many fields,
in 1923 created the Chapin Library at Williams College. Both these
men relied heavily upon the advice of Lathrop C. Harper, one of the
best-loved and, in his fields of Americana and incunabula, most knowl-
edgeable dealers in the country. Henry Walters, interested chiefly in
medieval manuscripts and incunabula, established his books as part of

the gallery he founded in Baltimore. William Andrews Clark, Jr., interested primarily in the Restoration and in Oscar Wilde, in 1926 deeded his collection—which became a part of the University in 1934—to the University of California at Los Angeles. And Carl H. Pforzheimer formed a strong collection of early English literature and Shelley material which was later given permanent form as a foundation for research.

William K. Bixby owned an extensive collection of autographs and many presentation copies of English nineteenth-century authors which was broken up by public and private sales. R. B. Adam's general English-literature collection was sold at auction, his Ruskins went to Yale, and his important books and manuscripts by and relating to Dr. Johnson were disposed of *en bloc* after his death to Donald Hyde. The twin peaks of the book boom of the 1920's were reached by the sales of the small, but choice, collection of early English literature formed by John L. Clawson in 1926 and of the books, rich in association items, of eighteenth- and nineteenth-century English authors collected by Jerome D. Kern in 1929. Some critics saw the extravagant speculation of the stock market reflected in the prices; others felt that rare books were at last realizing their potentials. The Kern sale, which realized a total of $1,729,462.50, set some records which have not been matched and which for a generation were looked upon with awe, amazement, and some horror.

Fashions in rare book collecting change, and, of course, several men seeking items in the same field create competition which in turn raises prices. When Henry E. Huntington, Henry C. Folger, William A. White, John L. Clawson, Charles W. Clark, and Carl H. Pforzheimer were actively buying early English literature, the market was strong. Their successors did not have their dollar-scornful appetite, and the prices of such books ebbed. During the middle 1920's, the authors of Dr. Johnson's circle, lauded by the enthusiastic A. Edward Newton, went from height to height, and the nineteenth century enjoyed a popularity not since accorded it. Early Americana, on the other hand, with some exceptions was not selling so well as earlier in the century, nor was the supply in the auction houses or in the hands of dealers so great.

In the boom period William M. Elkins brought together his important collections of Goldsmith and Dickens and began to buy early Americana, this later field not significantly increased until he acquired the pick of the Herschel V. Jones collection in 1940. At his death his books went to the Free Library of Philadelphia. Owen D. Young was one of the most enthusiastic plungers in the frantic book market; with his help Dr. A. A. Berg was able to buy the Young collection. Adding to it the complementary one of William T. H. Howe, Berg gave the collection to the New York Public Library in 1939, making that institution a major repository of English and American literature of the eighteenth and nineteenth centuries. Mr. and Mrs. Edward S. Harkness, patrons but never collectors, made major gifts to institutions, such as the Melk Abbey Gutenberg Bible to Yale and the large archive of Spanish-

American documents to the Library of Congress. Charles W. Clark, ranging wide with incunabula and French and English literature, bought during the peak years, as did the unrelated Dr. Roderick Terry and Seth Terry.

The depression years (1929-36) dealt the rare book collectors and dealers a severe blow. The new taxes, instituted by the New Deal, weighed heavily on the wealthy collector. A trend toward increased institutional buying and tax-deductible gifts to institutions was noticed. It was during the lean years that libraries like Harvard, Yale, Folger, and the New York Public, with endowments not too seriously crippled, were able to take advantage of the bargains offered to strengthen their collections.

The emergence of a new generation of rare-book-centered librarians who looked upon collectors as allies rather than competitors, who were recognized as authorities in their fields, and who were bibliophiles themselves further stimulated the flow of rare books to the institutional shelves of no-return. Following in the steps of such brilliant curators as Belle da Costa Greene at Morgan, Clarence S. Brigham at the American Antiquarian Society, Lawrence C. Wroth at John Carter Brown, Herbert Putnam at the Library of Congress, and Harry M. Lydenberg at the New York Public were the scholarly Joseph Q. Adams at Folger; Randolph G. Adams at Clements, one of the country's foremost spokesmen for rare books; the late William A. Jackson at Harvard, whose experience at the Chapin Library and his later work of compiling the catalog of the Pforzheimer Library gave him a background which few university rare book librarians had; John C. Wyllie at Virginia; Zoltan Haraszti at the Boston Public; and Julian C. Boyd, first at the Historical Society of Pennsylvania and later at Princeton.

There were some men who had begun their collections in the boom days and continued them thereafter, and a few who had the courage to begin when others stopped. Frank B. Bemis, who had been collecting great items of English and American literature for a generation, continued until his death, when his library was privately sold for the benefit of a hospital, first through Rosenbach and then through Goodspeed. John H. Scheide, who made a superb collection of books which influenced civilization (including a Gutenberg Bible, the first edition of *Pilgrim's Progress,* and significant Americana), left his library to his son William who has added to it—one of the few cases in recent years in which a major private library, now housed at Princeton, was handed down from father to son. Another father-son collection was the incomparable group of Indian narratives collected by Frank C. Deering, now in the possession of his son. The great Burns collection of John Gribbel was sold at auction, as were the fine romances of chivalry and Americana of John B. Stetson, Jr., the French eighteenth-century books of Mortimer L. Schiff (one of the few American libraries to be sold in London), Ellis Ames Ballard's Kiplings, and later the rich continental-type collections of fine books in fine bindings formed by Cortlandt Field Bishop and Lucius Wilmerding.

Rare book collections in the hands of an enthusiastic and knowl-
edgeable collector grow, almost without his realizing it, from a few
shelves of great books to a cohesive collection of real, scholarly importance. At some point the collection is so valuable or so significant
in its field that its owner must face the fact of its ultimate disposition.
With inheritance and income taxes high and family interest in the books
usually low, there has been an increasing inclination to make lifetime
gifts of such collections to institutions. In such a manner Lessing J.
Rosenwald gave his superb illustrated books from the fifteenth to the
twentieth century to the Library of Congress and, at the same time,
his extensive collection of prints and drawings to the National Gallery
of Art. George A. Plimpton gave his arithmetics, and Claude W. Kress
his books on business and economics, to Harvard University. Robert
Garrett's manuscripts, including the most important group of oriental
manuscripts in America, went to Princeton, as did eventually—by gift—
the Virginia Collection of Cyrus H. McCormick and the novels of
Morris L. Parrish and—by purchase—the rich Americana of Grenville
Kane.

John W. Garrett left his house and choice library as it was during
his lifetime to Johns Hopkins. Howard L. Goodhart's incunabula were
left to Bryn Mawr. Dr. Berg established his collection in the New York
Public Library, and to it also George Arents gave his collections of
books on tobacco and books in parts. Tracy W. McGregor virtually
created the rare book library of the University of Virginia with the bequest of his strong collection of Americana, and recently, to the same
institution, C. Waller Barrett has given major portions of his incomparable collection of American literature.

The carefree, anecdotal age of book collecting of which A. Edward
Newton was the spokesman was drawing to an end. Frank J. Hogan was
one of the last of his followers—an enthusiast during the depression.
Hogan's enthusiasm and the Newtonian spirit were communicated to
Mrs. Edward L. Doheny whose library at Camarillo, California—a
curious mixture of great books and manuscripts from Dr. Rosenbach
and of less great books reflecting the collector's personal likes—was
left to the Archdiocese of Los Angeles. By the time Newton died and
his books were dispersed at auction, the era which he chronicled had
come to an end. There were still a few wealthy men and women left in
the field who bought widely and expensively, such as Josiah K. Lilly,
Jr., whose collection of significant "firsts" was given to Indiana University; James F. Bell, whose early Americana formed the nucleus of
the rare book collection of the University of Minnesota; and Mrs. Roy
A. Hunt, whose botanical books went to the Carnegie Institute of Technology. Miss Clara Peck, whose outstanding collection of sporting
books has been promised to Transylvania College in Lexington, Kentucky, and Mrs. Landon K. Thorne, with a collection of many supreme
items of English literature, still have their books in their own possession.

These collectors had relied almost entirely for expertise upon dealers. But a new generation emerged who were their own experts. Outstanding as an Americanist is Thomas W. Streeter, whose flair and ingenuity were responsible for his unusual library of Americana. His railroad books were given to the American Antiquarian Society, and his huge Texas collection was sold to Yale. Wilmarth S. Lewis quickly became the outstanding authority on Horace Walpole and his period, and his house and the eighteenth-century collection will eventually go to Yale. Boies Penrose collected, and wrote, on East Indian voyages in particular and travel and navigation in general. Raphael Esmerian, a true connoisseur of bindings, created an impressive collection of them. Richard Gimbel amassed almost definitive collections in a number of fields: Dickens, Poe, Paine, and aeronautics. Donald and Mary Hyde are among the foremost scholars and own the major private collection of books and manuscripts of Dr. Johnson and his circle. Philip Hofer, as curator of the graphic arts at Harvard, has gathered a most important collection of books in his field for himself and the library. Harrison D. Horblit, specializing in works on navigation and related subjects, has become an authority on the history of science. And Dr. Frank T. Siebert, with a fine collection of books on the American Indian, knows his subject in bibliographical detail.

There have resulted a closer and more scholarly relationship between dealer, collector, and librarian, and a greater sharing of technical knowledge for the building up of a collection which may (and frequently does) end up on the shelves of an institution. Arthur A. Houghton, Jr.—who began his distinguished collecting career under the aegis of Dr. Rosenbach—after making incomparable collections of Keats and Spenser, gradually began to add to his choice library chiefly books which he learned Harvard would want. The classic example of this kind of collecting was Louis M. Rabinowitz, whose friendship for Yale and its librarian James T. Babb resulted in his buying most frequently for Yale or with Yale in mind. The same was true of the trio of Edward Eberstadt (the pioneer dealer in Western Americana), Babb, and the collector William Robertson Coe whose great library of western books was given to Yale.

In recent years one of the major booms in the book market has been in Western Americana. Important collections formed by C. G. Littell and W. J. Halliday have been sold at auction. Donald McKay's went to the American Antiquarian Society. Everett D. Graff gave his to the Newberry Library, and Everett L. DeGolyer's collection is maintained by his son as the DeGolyer Foundation in Dallas, Texas. At the same time a new interest in the history of science and medicine has pushed books in these fields into the limelight. Another DeGolyer collection, this time one of scientific books, went to the University of Oklahoma. The great ornithological library of Ralph Ellis is on the shelves of the University of Kansas whither other scientific collections have gravitated. The University of Wisconsin has, with other rare books, the Duveen chemistry collection, and the University of Chicago recently acquired the Herbert M. Evans great scientific "firsts." The outstanding scientific libraries of Bern Dibner and Robert B. Honeyman and the ornithological collection of H. Bradley Martin should not go unmentioned; as of 1964, they are still being added to by the owners.

A few individual collectors still buy the kind of "glamor" books which dominated the scene in the days of Morgan, Huntington, and Folger, and a few dealers specialize in the volumes which—because of fame, rarity, and/or beauty—command high prices and hence the headlines. The finest group of such books, rich in early English literature, was in the possession of Louis H. Silver of Chicago until his recent death when the collection was acquired by the Newberry Library. A similar collection has been formed by Raymond Hartz; Robert H. Taylor has specialized in Georgian and Victorian literature; an unusual group of medieval manuscripts has been gathered by William S. Glazier; and Paul Mellon has built an outstanding library dominated by Blake and color-plate books. The dealers who have been most active in carrying on the glamorous traditions of the past by paying record prices for superlative items are Hans P. Kraus and Dr. Rosenbach's successor, John Fleming.

Nonetheless, the trend—aided, even pushed, by the tax-deductible advantages of gifts and bequests to institutions—is toward the building up of institutional rare book libraries. The state-supported university libraries of the West and Middle West, adding state-appropriated funds to the benefactions of individuals, have been buying the bulk of the rare books which have come on the market. The University of Illinois, starting with almost no rare books a generation ago, is now, due to the stimulation of Professor H. F. Fletcher and the support of the Dean of Library Administration, Robert B. Downs, a major rare book repository. The collections of the University of California Library at Los Angeles, sparked by the magnetic enthusiasm of Lawrence C. Powell, librarian from 1944 to 1961, have grown at a snowballing rate.

Indiana University, with David A. Randall as its rare book librarian and the Lilly collection as its nucleus, has become an important factor in the rare book world. The collections of the University of Kansas under the guidance of its former director Robert Vosper (who has since become the librarian of the University of California at Los Angeles), and of the University of Kentucky under Lawrence S. Thompson, are both emerging into prominence. The Humanities Center at the University of Texas, sweeping the field of modern literature, has been one of the growth phenomena of recent years, and the rare book collections of Cornell, Syracuse, Stanford, and Rutgers have moved ahead rapidly in the same period.

To be sure, the older libraries of the country, most of them without public funds but with a longer tradition of interest, far larger collections, and hence a greater reservoir of friends or "Friends," have continued most successfully to increase and strengthen their holdings. The late William A. Jackson at Harvard was able imaginatively to record important accessions year after year. Yale, with its host of rare book experts on the faculty or staff of the library—following in the tradition of Professor Chauncey B. Tinker—has been aggressive in seeking collections and has found donors to give them. The Pierpont Morgan Library through the generosity of its Fellows and under the direction of Frederick B. Adams, Jr., is maintaining its policy of adding qualitatively to its holdings. Roland Baughman in charge of the special collections at Columbia, Howard H. Peckham at Clements, Stanley Pargellis at Newberry for nearly two decades, Thomas R. Adams at John Carter Brown, Louis B. Wright at Folger, Frederick R. Goff at the Library of Congress, Clifford K. Shipton at the American Antiquarian Society, John C. Wyllie at Virginia, and Howard C. Rice, Jr., at Princeton have all effectively improved, enlarged, and given leadership to the rare book collections under their care.

Small collections of high spots or books of specialized interest have been formed in many college and public libraries. Old libraries, rich in forgotten treasures, have been given new vigor: the venerable Library Company of Philadelphia under Edwin Wolf 2nd, the American Philosophical Society under Dr. William E. Lingelbach, the Watkinson Library by its merger with Trinity College, and the Pequot Library by its transfer to Yale. Old fields of collecting have been plowed with scholarly acumen and new fields exploited by dealers like Lew D. Feldman, Michael Papantonio, John S. Van E. Kohn, Richard S. Wormser, Philip C. Duschnes, Ralph Newman, George S. Goodspeed and his aide Michael Walsh, the brothers Eberstadt, Ernest J. Wessen, Warren Howell, Jacob Zeitlin and many others.

The Association of College and Research Libraries, the Grolier Club, the Bibliographical Society of America and other scholarly or local rare book clubs, and the host of Friends of various libraries have stimulated an understanding of the value of rare books and the delights of collecting them. A fruitful relationship has been worked out among private collectors, dealers, and rare book librarians to their mutual advantage. Inflation, a growing scarcity of great items, and a bubbling international market have raised prices beyond those of the 1920's; hence, new areas will have to be opened up for exploitation. The rare book has found a respected place in the libraries of America, and rare book collections will continue to grow as long as the funds and the books remain available, and as long as library personnel are properly trained to care for the materials under their charge.

Chapter III

Acquisition of Rare Materials

HOWARD H. PECKHAM

It is virtually impossible today for a library to begin a rare book collection from scratch, from absolute zero. The cost of acquiring an
initial corpus of books—a minimum number which could be called a
collection and be worth the attention of a scholar—is almost prohibitive. Most rare book collections are built on an initial gift of several
hundred or several thousand rarities from a private collector. There
is also a time element to consider. Even though a library may be
given a large sum of money with which to start a rare book collection,
the known rarities in the field selected are not likely to be available
immediately—or available for several years. Rare books are naturally
few in number, they are eagerly sought after, and patience is as necessary as willingness to pay. Fewer private collections come on the
market today to offer the newcomer an opportunity to collect in the
process of redistribution. At the least, usually a generation must pass
before a new collection may be fairly assessed.

On the other hand, a large library without a rare book collection is
likely to possess automatically a few or a good number of rarities
scattered on its shelves. They may be early local imprints, limited-
edition copies of certain fine books, first editions of subsequently
famous literary works, gift books, and the like. It can hardly be assumed, therefore, that any library interested in acquiring rare materials must start with nothing. The stimulation, indeed, is likely to come
from the discovery or realization that a few rarities are already on its
shelves. These areas of strength should help determine the course of
acquisition in the future.

The amount of money that can be devoted to collecting rarities
must be decided. One must cut one's pattern to the cloth. It is foolish
to decide to collect incunabula, seventeenth-century Americana, Edgar
Allan Poe, or western overland narratives on a slim budget; the prices
are simply too high to permit a growth in quantity. It is also important
that a definite sum or a percentage of appropriation be earmarked for

rare materials; otherwise, demands for current and popular materials (especially serials!) will take precedence and eat away funds once reserved for rarities, particularly if the funds have not been drawn on for a time. If rare book collecting is to be treated as a luxury, to be indulged in when appropriations are plentiful but cut off when times are stringent, then it is better not to adopt this stepchild. If an administrator cannot make a case for his collecting in hard times (when bargains may be available) as well as in flush times, he should confine himself to the obviously "useful" materials.

One of the first considerations in determining which rarities should be acquired is that they should be useful as source materials. This is especially true for history and biography. Source materials are the accounts of events or persons written by participants, eyewitnesses, or contemporaries and published shortly after the event took place or the subject died. In literature these materials are first editions, usually of the earliest published works of an author. In philosophy and science they are the first enunciations of a theory or the first reports of an experiment or discovery. Source material does not change; our interpretation of it does. Secondary works will continue to be written, probably by and for each new generation, but scholars return to examine the same source material with fresh insight and a revised or up-to-date vocabulary. Source materials are the gold bullion that support or redeem the paper currency of secondary works. They are not expended and they do not go out of date. When libraries prune their holdings in nonfiction, what they throw out are secondary works, interpretations that have become incorrect, biased, or outmoded. These are the titles of transient interest.

The second consideration in selecting rarities is priority. As indicated above, later editions and reprints seldom carry the importance or prestige of first editions. Reasons for this preference are not part of this essay; the fact is merely stated and must be accepted if a collection of rarities is to be formed. Some source materials, of course, were published in but one edition.

The next step is how to find what is wanted. There are in this country several hundred dealers in old and rare books, manuscripts, maps, and prints. They will be happy to send to libraries their catalogs and lists, which are issued several times a year. The librarian will find the names of these dealers and their specialties listed in the *Membership List* of the Antiquarian Booksellers' Association of America. A letter to as many as appear to stock materials in his field will put him on their mailing lists. There are other dealers in Europe and Asia whose catalogs may prove helpful. The librarian will find their advertisements in certain foreign periodicals, such as *The Book Collector* (London) or *Transactions of the Bibliographical Society* (London) among others.

Also, there are in the United States several firms that specialize in auction sales, usually during a season running from September through June. The three most active firms today (1964) are in New York City:

the Parke-Bernet Galleries, the Swann Galleries, and the American
Book Auction. In London, the firm of Sotheby and Company is the most
active in book sales, although Hodgson's and Christie's are firms
holding regular sales each season. In the fall of 1964, Sotheby acquired
a controlling interest in Parke-Bernet, and the details of this merger
were announced in the press. By placing annual subscriptions, libraries and individual collectors may receive the sales catalogs issued by
these firms.

From these sources the librarian will learn what is available and
receive his temptations. A few dealers may call on him in person
from time to time. But ordering also means selection and judgment.
The librarian must learn about priority values. I do not say "first
editions," because his focus may well be on a different order of first-
ness. At times he may be more concerned with first editions published
in America than true firsts, or with first illustrated editions, or autographed copies regardless of edition. In any event, the librarian will
need some familiarity in the subject field to learn which are the important sources and sufficient bibliographical information so as to
determine priority. Bibliographies also serve other purposes: by
describing books physically they inform one whether the copy under
consideration is fully complete; they supply the authors of anonymous
works when known; they contain notes about variations and origins;
and they may help provide correct entries for cataloging, although one
can never be certain that they are always accurate in this respect.

There are a few bibliographies basic to any effort at collecting rare
books. In the field of Americana, the general works are Charles Evans'
American Bibliography, listing all books printed in the United States
through 1800, and Joseph Sabin's *Dictionary of Books Relating to
America,* those printed up to the mid-nineteenth century.[1] For English
imprints there is Pollard and Redgrave, *Short-Title Catalogue of Books
Printed in England, Scotland, and Ireland, and of English Books Printed
Abroad, 1475-1640,* followed by Donald Wing's *Short-Title Catalogue of
Books Printed in England, Scotland, Ireland, Wales, and British Amer-
ica and of English Books Printed in Other Countries, 1641-1700.* The
Cambridge Bibliography of English Literature is the most comprehensive work in its field, and now in process of publication we have Jacob
Blanck's *Bibliography of American Literature.* J. T. Medina has fairly
well covered Spanish-American imprints in a series of studies. The
Gesamtkatalog der Wiegendrucke is the most extensive catalog of incunabula (so far as it has been published to date) and is gradually su-
perseding Hain's *Repertorium* and Copinger's *Supplement.* Catalogs in
book form of major libraries are also useful bibliographies, such as
those of the Library of Congress and of the British Museum.

---

[1] Joseph Sabin, *Dictionary of Books Relating to America, from Its Discovery to the
Present Time* (29v.; New York: Sabin, 1868-92; Bibliographical Soc. of America, 1928-
36). Beginning with Volume 20, its scope is limited due to the lapse of publication between 1892 and 1928.

All kinds of national, regional, and topical bibliographies exist; the Winchell *Guide to Reference Books* (and supplements) classifies them and provides brief annotations about their contents, use, and the like. There are also special bibliographies: those relating to a printer, author, city, state, region, period, or topic. All those relating to the area covered by one's collection should be purchased, insofar as the library can afford them. The purpose of any and all of these bibliographies is to acquaint the librarian, first, with relevant titles in addition to those he already has and, second, to verify titles he is cataloging.

A final word should be said about preparations and aids. Not all the required information has been published. It is wise, therefore, to become acquainted with private collectors or dealers who are specialists in one's field. They are likely to have picked up various bits of information about books and editions that one should know, and they often enjoy sharing their knowledge.

Equipped with some tools of the trade, the librarian should be ready to make actual purchases. When a sales catalog is received, it must be searched for titles that may be wanted. Ordinarily, these are checked by the librarian or curator, then searched to see whether they are already owned. Before ordering from the catalogs of dealers, it is important to read their notes, which usually appear in fine print. Here will be found the physical description of the copy, the identity of the edition, the marks of previous ownership, and so on. If the title is one wanted (according to the notes or bibliographies) and is the edition wanted (first or otherwise), then the librarian should concern himself about its physical condition. Is it all there, with no plates or pages missing? Is it an ex-library copy stamped in indelible ink or with pages perforated or stamped on the fore edge to show former ownership? These factors detract from the desirability and value of the book. As for the binding, or lack of one, thought should be given to the cost of repairing or rebinding. The librarian is going to handle and administer rare books, and the books must look the part.

Private collectors and librarians may part company over this matter of the most preferable binding. If a book was issued sewn in wrappers or without stiff covers, the private collector will prize a copy in that condition and have a box made to protect it. If the first edition was bound in paper boards, he will prefer that. The librarian may well pause here and remember that he collects for use by others. A sturdy eighteenth-century calf binding, or one in modern morocco, may justifiably have more appeal to him than a naked, unprotected copy. The latter may be fine to display in an exhibition case under glass, but it is too fragile for anything more than occasional use.

The catalog description may also mention a bookplate or the name of a previous owner. This kind of mark does not detract from the value of an old book and may well enhance it. If the copy offered bears the name of "George Washington," one will have to pay at least $1,500 for it, even though in unmarked form it is only a dollar book. The fame of the previous owner is certainly a factor in price. Similarly, if that owner has added marginal notes, these are not a disfigurement but an adornment of added value.

Assuming that the physical condition of the book is satisfactory, the librarian must next consider the price. Serving as guides here there are three sources. One is the priced catalogs of other dealers already received, from which comparisons may be made. Another is the annual volume with cumulated indexes of *American Book-Prices Current,* containing the prices realized at auctions by all books sold for $5 or more during a season; the English *Book-Prices Current* is a similar compilation for books realizing more than £1. These annual volumes also contain prices realized by manuscripts, maps, and broadsides. A quicker way of getting part of this information, for books sold by Parke-Bernet, is to subscribe to their priced lists, which are sent out after each sale. The other source, but only for Americana published after 1650, is Wright Howes's *U.S.IANA, 1650-1950,* a compilation of selected titles with estimates of their scarcity and value.[2] Continued experience in reading catalogs and ordering gradually helps to give one a sense of approximate values for books in one's field.

If priority, condition, and price are right, the next step is to order, and order promptly. One reason for the separate organization of rare book collections is to speed the process of searching and ordering. In large libraries the daily accumulation of catalogs of recent publications, serials, and old books and the consequent delay in selecting and searching are almost fatal to procurement of rare books. Even though one orders within twenty-four hours of receipt of the catalog, one must be prepared to suffer disappointments. Private collectors often use the telephone (and so should the librarian on occasion); customers happen in to a bookstore from the street and walk off with what a library wants; and at times a dealer staggers the mailing of his catalogs to favor his best customers first. Even if he does mail all at once, the customers living near to his store's location receive their copies first. So time is of the essence. Searching of a catalog and prompt decision take precedence over other activities of a rare book division.

Nearly all orders should be requests for material to be sent "on approval." This is a safeguard to the librarian on two points: he may check the accuracy of the dealer's description of condition and of the title itself. Sometimes dealers do not collate their wares, and upon close examination the buyer may find pages or plates missing. Again, a dealer may use a shortened title or a different entry in cataloging a book which leads a rare book curator to believe that he does not have the item; but upon arrival of the book, the full title is found to be a duplicate of one already in the library. In either of these cases, the book may be returned to the dealer with an explanation. If the book is as represented, then it should be accepted and paid for. There is no excuse for delay in payments or returns, and the penalty is that dealers

---

[2]A second, revised, edition was published in 1962.

will be reluctant to send books on approval to institutions that cannot seem to make up their minds. Indeed, when a dealer receives in the same mail an order "on approval" and another order outright, he cannot be blamed for favoring the latter. However, most dealers allow returns for any error in cataloging or for subsequent discovery that the new item is a duplicate, within a certain time limit.

Buying at auction requires special knowledge. Obviously, one cannot make returns except in instances of gross misrepresentation. Items offered in auction catalogs are put on display before the sale. Moreover, the auction house "does not warrant the correctness of description, genuineness, authenticity or condition" of the books and manuscripts. *Caveat emptor!* One may bid in one of two ways: either directly to the auction house by mail (usually a form is enclosed in each catalog) or by using a dealer as agent who will add a charge of 10 percent as his commission. The danger of bidding by mail is inherent in the quoted statement above. On the other hand, if a bid or bids total around $50, it is almost an imposition to ask a dealer to attend the sale at the risk of earning $5 for his effort. Individual items or small lots, where the librarian feels himself on safe ground in accepting the catalog description, may be bid for by mail. But valuable books or a large number of items should be entrusted to a dealer; his commission is one's insurance.[3]

Visits, on occasion, to the offices of dealers may be advantageous. Besides the benefit of personal acquaintance and discussion of needs, the librarian may run across desirable titles recently acquired by the dealer and before he has cataloged them for general sale. The same may be said for a visit with European dealers abroad, but whether the expense of such a trip can be justified by advantageous purchases is questionable unless a large sum of money is to be spent.

A word of caution is in order on the matter of haggling. Bookdealers are not rug peddlers; they do not name a price as a starting point for negotiation. Their prices are usually the result of careful judgment and long experience. It is hardly polite, to say the least, to order an item and then begin an argument about the price. If one believes the item is overpriced, one should not order it. If others agree, the dealer will discover he is asking too much. On the other hand, after the lapse of a few months, it is not improper to write to a dealer in the following tenor: "In your catalog of————you listed————at $500. If it has not sold at this price, and you would consider a reduction, we are still interested in the title." If the dealer still has the item, he may be glad of an opportunity to move it at a discount. If he has sold it, he will be even happier to tell you—and you must revise your judgment of what that item is worth.

Occasionally a private collector or librarian strives to become a "smart buyer" who never pays the cataloged price. This is a dubious

---

[3]The best recent statement on buying at auction is John Carter's "Book Auctions," *Library Trends*, 9, no.4:471-82 (April 1961).

reputation to acquire. Some dealers meet these hagglers on special deals by inflating their asking price and reducing it under pressure to the normal figure. A more serious consequence is that the haggler is never offered a choice item first. Indeed, he usually gets it last. A dealer has remarked, "When I take an item to Mr.————, you may be sure that I have failed to sell it anywhere else." Such a reputation is virtually ruinous for ambitious collecting.

Gifts are usually a boon, yet sometimes a problem. It is admittedly difficult to decline gracefully something one does not want. Still, it must be done, to avoid spreading one's self thin. To obtain gifts one wants requires some effort. The librarian must cultivate collectors who are acquiring the type of material needed by the library. Since both have a common interest, they will have a natural tie. The librarian can make the collector feel at home in the library. The latter may be glad to make use of his bibliographies, or order printed catalog cards through the library. He should be invited to the library's social functions and certain conferences. This is not calculated covetousness, but an extension of courtesies to a kindred soul. Most collectors feel that they are doing something worthwhile and hope that their collections may remain intact and beneficial to others. The idea of depositing them in a library is likely to appeal to many donors.

Want lists are of little use in rare book collecting, beyond indicating to the librarian that in a given field his library is weakly represented. If it is, he may wish to concentrate on book hunting for a while. The want list is a quick reference to what the library lacks. One use of such a list is to focus attention on lacunae in a sequence. For instance, certain historical controversies have elicited arguments and rebuttals that may run to a dozen or more titles. In preparing a want list, the librarian learns exactly which ones are lacking, and he then initiates a special search to find them so as to complete the sources on a particular incident. But sending a want list to a dealer usually ends in disappointment; the library may be fortunate if the dealer can supply 1 to 2 percent of the titles. A dealer will be glad to look out for the other titles and give the interested library the first opportunity to buy—*after* he has managed to find them. The same want list should not be sent to more than two or three dealers.[4] If the librarian scatters the list, he is in danger of increasing the prices he will have to pay, since several dealers will be bidding against one another to get the titles for which they think they have a sure resale.

If want lists produce little response, and if purchases must be selected from what dealers have to offer, buying must unavoidably be of scattered items. In any one year the acquisitions are likely to be miscellaneous, rather than concentrated in subject matter. This is not to say that such buying is haphazard. Every new title that fits among

---

[4]Some librarians have found it wise to restrict the want list to one dealer at a time, for by giving an exclusive to a dealer, better results may be realized. However, this procedure is often dependent on the nature of the want list and the specialty of the dealer.

related items is a proper and enriching addition. The librarian cannot
expect to establish a pattern of acquisitions with one year's purchases,
or two or three years' purchases, because he is adding to a variety of
subjects and sequences in the library. Each addition strengthens some
part of the collection. But the circumstances of the market force the
librarian's buying to be opportunistic. This may be all that can be done.

Moreover, the rare book librarian cannot budget his money so as to
spend so much each month, because he is not buying an article that is
being manufactured. If he lacks a title, he must order when it is offered—not when he might like to buy it. If he does not order then, he
may not have a second opportunity for several years. In fact, if a long-
desired title becomes available, even at a price that takes a quarter or
a third of an annual appropriation, it may be wise to purchase it. Admittedly this is a difficult decision, but there may be times when such
courage is a mark of administrative ability. In seeking rare books, the
librarian admittedly cannot often exercise much initiative, though there
are still some who manage to make important "finds." Most attics of
old families have been pretty well cleaned out. It is impossible to make
a house-to-house canvass, and antique shops are hardly worth the
searching time. The wise librarian *can* cultivate collectors with a view
to purchasing their collections or persuading them to become donors.

A different approach, just as obligatory, is to study various fields
of collecting for the purpose of identifying and establishing source materials not yet recognized as such. Bibliographers have not found
everything; there has never been a complete bibliography. Rare book
librarians render a genuine service to scholars by discovering new
sources for the latter to use. This may be the chief reason why some
librarians find scholarly associations more congenial than library associations.

In the field of manuscripts, initiative is more often rewarded. Old
families will keep letters longer than books. It sometimes pays to
search for descendants of persons who were important in the library's
field of interest. A librarian who sits at his desk and buys only what
is brought to his attention by catalogs or dealers' visits is not doing a
full job. He should feel obliged to do some intelligent searching. A
related duty is to find additional funds, if not material; and this is
usually accomplished through the aid of an organization of library
Friends. Such enterprise is discussed more fully by John Parker in
Chapter X.[5]

The rare book librarian cultivates or recognizes certain attitudes
toward acquisition that will inevitably distinguish him from the head of
a public or college library. I have mentioned the impossibility of bud-
geting a library's expenditures so as to enjoy an even flow throughout

---

[5]See also Frances J. Brewer's article, "Friends of the Library and Other Benefac-
tors and Donors," *Library Trends*, 9, no.4:453-65 (April 1961) and the volume edited
by Sarah L. Wallace, *Friends of the Library* (Chicago: American Library Association,
1962).

the year, and the opportunistic buying that must prevail over concentrated effort in a single direction. There are other principles to be kept in mind. First is the fact of selection. One must constantly exercise discrimination and judgment. The rare book librarian is not often able to buy everything in a given field or everything by a given author. He may not be able to afford a "special collection." He looks for the most important, the significant, the best, the most desirable. He may never have funds enough to buy even these selected few; so he must select wisely those items which will benefit his library's collection the most.

He need not be troubled by the possibility that no one will use these books immediately. Librarians are buying for posterity, for permanent preservation, not merely to satisfy the current fashion of interest. These tides of scholarly preference ebb and flow. Spanish-Americana, for instance, is not the field of interest it was twenty years ago—but it will come back. The American decorative arts are popular now, but in the future some other field will have gained prominence. Just because no one in the vicinity of one's library is interested in the flora of Japan is no good reason for not building a collection, provided you have a start—some future botanist is likely to find it very useful. Indeed, the truth of the matter is that normally the collection must precede the interest. If the librarian develops the best collection of scarce picaresque novels, *then* someone will make use of them.

In the rare book field, collecting is the librarian's prime responsibility. All other duties—personnel, cataloging, serving readers, procuring space, and the like—are secondary. He is working in a maze of designs, striving for the impossible completion of a grand composition. This is the challenge, the absorption, the fun, of acquisition. It is significant work, too. A piece of wisdom to be borne in mind was given by Lawrence S. Thompson, Director of Libraries at the University of Kentucky:

> Future generations will not remember present-day librarians for their organizational charts, their surveys, their classification and pay plans, their ingenious fanfold forms—however necessary they may be for day-by-day operations. Scholars of the twenty-first century will measure the accomplishments of the librarian not so much by his techniques in dealing with a twentieth century public but by the collections he built. [6]

---

[6] Lawrence S. Thompson, "Of Bibliological Mendicancy," *College and Research Libraries,* 14, no.4:378 (Oct. 1953).

Chapter IV

Organization of a Collection

ROLAND O. BAUGHMAN

The usefulness of books in libraries is ordinarily dependent on their characteristics of subject, date, and authority; their classification into accessible order for the purposes of study and research is, for the most part, a matter of determining and codifying the details of those characteristics. The potential reader is thereby enabled to go directly to the shelves for the materials he needs, where, in theory at least, he will also find on the same shelf or near at hand—because of the classifier's work—other texts that are related to his interest.

But these are by no means the only dimensions which books may have, and in the case of "rare books," especially, elements that deserve priority may have little or nothing to do with textual content. Some peculiarity or particularity of issue, for example, or some specific feature of provenance, of physical condition, and so on, may give singular interest to a representative of an otherwise ordinary edition, or enhance the interest of an important one. In such cases normal subject classification methods are seldom adequate, and the librarian is faced with the responsibility of determining which features shall be emphasized.

Collections that have been acquired *en bloc* present their own special problems. Even those which have been built around well-defined themes, and in which, therefore, subject factors may be expected to dominate, call for complex considerations. Such unit groups may merit the designation "rare" or "special" for any one or more of a variety of reasons: completeness of subject coverage, presence of individual rarities, source, condition of acquisition, or because they represent specific interest or exceptional knowledge on the part of the original collector. Indeed, a collection that is entirely without intrinsic value may possess importance merely because its former owner was important. When, as often happens in institutional libraries, unit collections are acquired, a whole series of interrelated decisions must be reached. It is to this particular side of rare book technique that the present chapter is devoted.

UNIT COLLECTION VERSUS DISPERSAL

The basic decision that must be made first of all in assimilating a
newly acquired collection is whether it is to be maintained as an intact
unit, or whether it should be mingled with other books of like subject,
thereby enhancing and being enhanced by the existing contents of the library. The principal concern here has to do with the immediate source
of the collection—whether it has come by gift or by purchase. If it has
come by gift or bequest, the terms under which it was accepted become
paramount and must be honored, and these may stipulate that the collection be preserved intact. But if, on the other hand, no such stipulation has been made, or if the collection has been purchased with institutional funds, the librarian should feel quite free to organize it along
lines that seem to him to be most logical and efficient, being careful to
give full regard to the possibility that dispersal may destroy something
that cannot be recovered. It may also lead to complications by the cre-
ation of duplicates in the general files. Questions relating to the propriety of disposing of duplicating gift or bequest copies will be discussed below.

Indeed, for a number of reasons, dispersal may not be the best solution even when permissible; and here is the place to stress the fact
that, in rare book libraries with closed stacks, the objections to maintaining collections in separate units and in orders different from the
library's primary classification system are difficult to support by
logic. In reality it makes little difference *how* books are arranged on
the shelves of a closed stack *insofar as the efficiency of reader service
is concerned,* always providing that the arrangement is controlled by an
effective location system.

It must be assumed, of course, that the rare book division has its
own reading room where its books are consulted under surveillance,
and that there is not stack access or shelf consultation by readers, the
books being brought from the stack and returned to their places after
use by rare book division attendants. (If these basic provisions have
not been made, there is little valid reason for having a rare book division in the first place.) It must be assumed further that there is an
adequate catalog of the rare books, complete with all necessary subject
headings and cross references. With these fundamentals provided for,
the advantages of having books classified by subject may become secondary to other considerations.

Freedom from the *necessity* for subject classification makes it
easier for the rare book librarian to do what eventually every such librarian *must* do in any case, namely, create unit collections of his own
devising that may have little reference to textual content, in order to
facilitate proper handling of books which represent like problems of
storage and preservation: incunabula, book manuscripts, association
copies, extra-illustrated works, early American imprints, fine or historical bindings, and the like. This does not differ essentially in tech-

nique from preserving collections as units for reasons of provenance, which likewise may leave subject content entirely out of consideration.

The location symbols which render such special files workable from the point of view of reader service need not be complicated. If the staff member understands that, for example, "Peterson Collection: Scilly Islands" refers to a certain part of a certain collection, and that the part referred to is arranged on the shelves by imprint date and by catalog entry within a given year, he has everything he needs on a properly filled-out call slip for locating any book in that particular file. The special problems concerning pamphlet volumes, broadsides, books of abnormal size or shape, and the like need not detain us here, because they are common to all systems of classification.

It is obviously within the moral right of a donor to seek to control the destiny of his gift or bequest collection by setting down any conditions he may desire pertaining to it; it is equally within the right of an institution to accept or reject a collection that is subject to inordinately difficult or costly conditions. Libraries are becoming more and more careful in accepting gifts on terms which prejudice basic policies, and donors, too, are learning that overly restrictive conditions of gift may in the long run defeat their own purposes. In many instances where it is possible to discuss the matter, the zone of difference between what the donor wants and what it is possible to supply can be narrowed to the point where the main objectives of both parties can be achieved. But bequests are another matter, because it is seldom possible to discuss the terms under which collections are to be bequeathed; quite frequently institutions are informed of what had been in the donor's mind only when his will is probated. The best that can be done in the face of difficult bequest conditions is to weigh their long-term implications against the research usefulness and monetary value of the materials— and accept or reject the collection on the basis of those deliberations.

For one reason or another, however, a gift or bequest may be accepted even though the terms are difficult or contrary to policy. When this is the case, it must be done with utter honesty. If the conditions stipulate a permanent arrangement, such as special quarters or a special curator, there can be no reservation in anyone's mind as to how long a time the word "permanent" implies. All this may seem to belabor the obvious, but there is a substantial element of self-interest in these remarks. The simple truth is that gifts and bequests are an important factor in the growth of most research libraries, and potential donors can quickly become cynical about an institution that has earned a reputation for ignoring or forgetting promises made when gifts have been accepted. The *legality* of an institution's actions is not the issue here; we are concerned only with their ultimate effect on donor relations.

(In passing, it should be noted that agreement often can be reached with prospective donors, whereby excessively strict controls are understood to have a stated terminal date. For example, a donor may wish to have his collection closed to use or housed in some unusual

way—such as in his own home—during his lifetime or for some other
finite and reasonable period. Such conditions are in general entirely
workable, and almost any institution can undertake to carry out the
terms of the agreement, in the knowledge that eventually the full interests of scholarship will be served.)

Fortunately for librarians and readers, the great majority of gift
collections come without insurmountable complications. The most
which a donor is likely to ask—unless his collection is of exceptional
notability—is that his gift be maintained as a unit. Quite often even
this stipulation will be softened, after discussion, to identification by
special bookplate, without the need for separate shelving. Under the
latter arrangement, no unusual problems will face the librarian.

SPECIAL ROOMS

To be maintained as a separate unit a collection does not necessarily have to be housed in a separate room, but conditions of gift or bequest not infrequently specify such rooms. Conditions of this kind
constitute just about the most difficult and costly arrangement that can
be devised, particularly if special curatorial service is stipulated. The
dollar figure against which this requirement must be weighed should include the capital investment involved in the construction and furnishing
of the room (even if it already exists), as well as the budgetary costs
of the curator, janitorial service, and utilities. In a very few fortunate
institutions, where both the original building plans and the institutional
policy have included provisions for such rooms and where fiscal pres-
sures are easy, or in cases where the gift collection has come with fully
endowed support, the costs will not represent an immediate problem.

In the face of continued growth, however, no building is ultimately
large enough, and the earnings of endowed funds have an embarrassing
tendency to fluctuate as economic conditions change. For the most
part, the setting aside of special rooms can be justified—and properly
carried out—only in the cases of the few "crown jewel" collections
which every library has a right to take a full measure of pride in possessing. But it may be well to add that there can be no gainsaying the
powerful attraction which such facilities have for donors, because they
represent the closest possible approach to the personal care which a
collector can give his own books. It is therefore adding difficulty to
difficulty for an institution to rule out by unalterable policy, as some
do, the acceptance of special room collections, particularly if donor
support for general purposes is being sought.

It may occur to some readers that the above lays heavy emphasis
on the role of the donor and the need to preserve his favor. It does,
indeed, and for the reason that, in this day of federal leniency toward
income tax deductions for gifts that benefit educational institutions, the
acquisition of costly books and manuscripts through the action of donors is at a peak. Especially for institutions that do not have public

tax support, this is a fortunate situation, and one which must be used to the fullest advantage of scholarship, for no one knows how long the favorable leniency will be continued. Since World War II, it has become increasingly difficult for library budgets to keep abreast of rising bread-and-butter costs, and the acquisition of expensive collections would, for the most part, be quite unfeasible if it were not for the donor interest that is being fostered by tax rulings. And if, in addition to giving his collection, a donor can be persuaded to provide an endowment for its continuing development, the ultimate has been achieved. Other things being equal, even a modest endowment that is available throughout the future can do wonders in supplying the background materials needed to enhance the research usefulness of a collection of individual treasures.

GIFT APPRAISALS

At this point we encounter the moot matter of enabling a donor to obtain the optimum legal benefit from his gift by way of tax deductions. *Any manual of procedures for this should be written by the most competent tax lawyer available,* who would do well to work closely with federal and state tax bureaus. The manual would, moreover, be subject to change with every change in the laws governing deductions for such gifts. This, obviously, is a matter in which no mere librarian should meddle. The present writer, at any rate, lacks the temerity to do more than set down in the broadest possible terms the policy of his own institution.

Actual appraisals of valuable collections and single items should be made only by disinterested third parties who are recognized as reputable experts in current book values and in the subject area of the particular material in hand, *and who are prepared to defend their evaluations.* Happily, the city in which the writer's institution is located is well supplied with such experts, so that it is always possible to refer the donor, upon request, to at least two individuals for consideration. In order to keep the transaction as simple and straightforward as possible, the cost of the appraisal may properly be borne by the donor, in which case, as matters now stand, the fee becomes a part of the gift. A formal statement of recommended library policy regarding appraisals was submitted by the Committee on Appraisals and adopted at Oberlin College, July 7, 1961, when the Rare Books Section met. A copy of this statement is reprinted in the Appendix.

In the case of collections and items of low monetary worth we will sometimes furnish "estimates of approximate value," but only when the figures are so modest as to present no conceivable doubt of their defensibility. For moderately rare materials we may go so far as to quote the current price of a particular item as revealed in auction records or catalogs of well-known dealers. Even so, we are careful *not* to declare a given book to have a specific value; we say only that similar copies have sold for such-and-such an amount, citing in full the sources of our information.

At first glance this procedure may appear to be a shameless begging of the question, but to anyone who gives the matter sober thought it will be clear that the least an institution owes its donors is protection from tax trouble. To encourage, even in the guise of a favor, the slightest prospect of involving a benefactor—and one's institution, if not one's self—in litigation is small thanks for a gift. If a librarian states that a specific volume has a specific value, he should be prepared to go before the tax authorities and prove it. And even when there can be no doubt of his competence to evaluate books, if he is an interested party to the gift there may be those who will question his declaration.

CLASSIFICATION

It would be reasonable to suppose that a collection developed by a specialist around some particular subject would offer few difficulties of classification. Actually, however, a privately formed collection of the literature pertaining to, for example, the history of books and bookmaking would, by the very nature of things, be altogether different in certain details from one formed by a librarian following an equally definite plan. The former would almost certainly contain a great deal of tangential, peripheral, and incidental material which the latter would not include because it would already be available to him under some other subject classification and because specific pertinencies would be taken care of in the catalog. The private collector would have no such resources at his command in the way of general reference and contributory material, and his library on book history might well include works like Sarton's *History of Science,* Singer's *History of Technology,* catalogs, separate issues of scholarly journals containing relevant articles, popular archaeological writings such as those of Ceram, Gordon, and Cottrell, book collectors' periodicals, and the like.

Two courses are open to the librarian in dealing with the problem which this difference of approach presents. If the terms of gift are adamant, he must classify the collection as it stands, which becomes, because of its varied coverage, a reflection of the general collection, though heavily weighted on the side of the donor's special interest. Books that are duplicated in the library system are handled just as though they were not duplicated.

It is not unusual, however, for the separate collection stipulation to be worded in such a way as to provide the librarian with some leeway, which it is proper for him to use in the best interests of the collection that is no longer a private and personal possession but a part of an active research library. For example, the terms of gift may contain some such statement as: "The rare books and manuscripts in my collection are to be preserved as a unit." In the absence of any knowledge of contrary intent, this may be interpreted as limiting the unit collection to important works and permitting the removal of secondary materials to the general files. *It would be improper to take this interpretation,* however, if it is known or suspected that the donor viewed *all* of his books as forming a homogeneous unit; the librarian who feels any doubt whatever should preserve the collection's integrity—and his own— above all other considerations.

RESTRICTIONS

Unit collections that have been purchased with institutional funds should not be subject to restrictions, unless the purchase was contingent on them, either in price or in availability. It is one thing to accept restrictions on a gift collection, but it is another matter entirely to expend institutional funds in a way that limits the institution's authority over the material purchased. This stipulation, of course, presupposes that the institution has set up, or intends to do so, a department specifically entrusted with caring for rare books and manuscripts, so that such items acquired in unit purchases will be properly administered.

PROBLEMS OF DISPERSAL

The problems that arise in connection with the dispersal of unit collections, though multitudinous, require for their solution little more than good common sense, a reasonably sound knowledge of rare books, and a reluctance to create difficulties for one's successors. The principal areas for concern are: (1) the need for a record of the original contents of a collection as formed by the donor; (2) procedures for handling duplicates of works already in the files, together with the question of the propriety of disposing of such duplicates acquired in gift or bequest collections; and (3) the distinguishing of materials that should go to the rare book division from those that would serve a better purpose in the main collection.

Recording the Collection

The first point, the need for recording the contents of any collection that is to be dispersed (especially if it contains materials that, when classified in a standard way, will be shelved apart from the main group), becomes no problem at all if a checklist of the collection has been or is to be compiled. In the case of a relatively small collection this can be a simple author-title list, to be filed with other documents pertaining to the gift. Larger collections containing a substantial proportion of rarities can be accommodated by running off an extra card for each item at the time of cataloging; this should be held as a record file in the rare book division or in any other office of the library designated as the repository for such documents. Book material that is held uncataloged should at least be listed, and vertical file material should be sorted and described in the gift dossier.

The value of this kind of record will be readily appreciated. In the case of a small or altogether heterogeneous collection of rarities, the content of the original gift can be quickly reconstructed. In the case of a subject collection that once contained a wide variety of peripheral, tangential, incidental, or contributory material, scholarly use will be greatly facilitated by references that record the special knowledge which the original collector had so painstakingly amassed; the mere fact that a certain item was once a part of the subject collection may lead a reader to a source that might otherwise have escaped him.

Such records should be considered in connection with all dispersed collections, even though special processing procedures are to be followed in order to bring out in the catalog the obscure relationships of certain materials to the subject collection. Sometimes, of course, these records will be deemed unnecessary, for gift collections may vary widely in interest and merit. Here, again, the attitude of the donor or his heirs and friends must be considered. Especially when large libraries are the beneficiaries, the apprehension that gifts will be lost in the great mass of materials already present must be counteracted.

Duplicates in Gift Collections

It is a rare thing for a gift or bequest collection to consist entirely of works that are new to the beneficiary library. As noted above, the duplicates contained in such a collection present no great problem unless the collection is to be dispersed, in which case the duplicates are subject to a variety of handling procedures: (1) they can be cataloged in such a way as to bring out their special interest to the original collection; (2) they can be cataloged as second copies; (3) they can be held uncataloged as reserve copies against the day when the cataloged ones need replacement; or (4) they can be disposed of by sale, gift, or exchange.

The first possibility is preferable in certain instances; in a library where an effort has been made to bring together all of the published work of Arthur Rackham, for example, a single issue of the *Ladies' Home Journal* for December, 1925, should be cataloged for his contribution, even though the library has a full run of that magazine elsewhere on its shelves. The second possibility, cataloging second copies to be shelved alongside the originals, probably should not be adopted except in instances of undoubted usefulness—in cases of questionable usefulness the third possibility is preferable. The sale or exchange of duplicates that have been acquired by gift should not be undertaken without the donor's express approval; *this entire matter should be cleared with him at the time the gift is being arranged,* and his permission to dispose of duplicates should be a matter of record, preferably a part of the article of gift. When bequests are involved, the situation is fraught with even graver concern. The librarian who authorizes the disposal of duplicates and other unneeded materials from the bequest collections of recently deceased public figures should be very sure of his ground, for he may be risking serious criticism from other prospective donors.

In any case, the dispersal of duplicates from well-known collections is a delicate matter. When it is done, each volume that is released should bear some sort of permanent notation that authorizes its departure from the collection. The librarian may not know until much too late the damage that can be done to his institution's reputation among collectors by those who, for lack of reasonable assurance to the contrary, assume carelessness in the preservation of the unity of a great collection. This assumption is not always easy to combat, for the reason—among many—that owners themselves not infrequently release volumes bearing their bookplates prior to presenting or selling their collections to libraries. I myself have had occasion to purchase items that had been so released from unit collections at my institution, and I have likewise had occasion to communicate with other libraries before purchasing items from collections that I knew to be in those libraries, because the volumes contained no evidence of authorized release.

One large university follows a different practice and removes all signs of ownership, *ex libris,* and the like when a book is to be discarded. This is done so that the future buyer will not know that the book has been discarded by the institution. There may be cases where this would be difficult to accomplish, and the danger of making a categorical rule in matters of this kind is evident.

Identification of Important Items

Collectors who aim at completeness for their subject libraries hope to acquire not only the obvious, outstanding rarities, but the lesser-known materials as well. When both kinds of books are combined with the usual content of standard works in a subject collection, the task of the librarian who must make the decisions by which the collection is to be divided is exacting. No experienced librarian, of course, will have trouble in identifying either the obvious rarities or the standard texts, and decisions for isolating these for the rare book or the working files will be easily reached. On the other hand, the obscure minutiae of the collection, the out-of-the-way items whose significance is known only to the specialist, require careful thought. The importance to printing history of a quite ordinary-looking twelvemo edition of Sallust, published in Edinburgh by Gulielmus Ged in 1739, might be overlooked by a cataloger who failed to heed the fine print in Latin at the bottom of the title page, thereby missing the fact that this represents Ged's first successful attempt to produce a complete book by means of his newly invented stereotyping process.

The point to be stressed is that each volume in a subject collection must be closely scrutinized so that its relevance to the subject, if any exists, will be found—the librarian always remembering that nearly any collector who is a free agent will acquire attractive items that are outside his avowed field of interest. It is the latter point which causes the greatest difficulty for the cataloger of a subject collection and makes the listing of the collection as received so needful.

RELATION OF NEW COLLECTION TO EXISTING HOLDINGS

There are three principal categories into which new collections can be sorted: those representing essentially new subject fields; those which add strength to existing fields; and those which simply provide association copies of works already present. The last-named category presents few difficulties of organization, because the reasons for acquiring the collection in the first place should dictate that it be preserved as a unit; duplication will then be an advantage rather than a problem, for the reason that ordinary reader use can largely be directed away from the association copies. *It should, in fact, be standard practice to duplicate in the general files all working texts of which association or other unusual copies are held in the rare book collections.* Nevertheless, since the possession of an association file which does not materially augment the library's subject content is chiefly a matter of pride and propriety, there will be the natural compulsion to maintain it in commensurate physical condition, involving unusual expenses for renovation, repair, rebinding, protective cases, and perhaps special housing as well.

Collections which do not represent entirely new subjects, but which provide added strength to existing fields, are apt to contain a large percentage of duplication. Many of the problems discussed above will arise to a greater degree in connection with this kind of collection than with other types. If it can be dispersed, questions related to the weeding of unneeded items and to their proper disposal will have to be resolved. If the collection must remain a unit, it will assume the nature of an association file, with complications arising from its admixture of a high ratio of items needed for everyday reference with those of limited use.

If, however, the new collection represents an essentially new field in the library, and if that field is considered to have relevance to the library's larger program, several points requiring decisions will come up—decisions which will vary according to various institutional policies. Important among these points will be the implied obligations to augment the collection as opportunities arise, and to keep it current as new relevant material is published. If it is decided that the new field is to be developed, and if the collection has not come with endowed support, such acquisitions either will call for additional budgetary commitments or will be made at the expense of the existing acquisitions program. There is also the question of whether newly acquired current material, purchased by means of institutional funds in support of a collection that cannot be dispersed, should go to the general files, or be included in the new collection, thus providing a single service point for the subject group.

I cannot refrain from injecting here my own strong prejudice against mixing rare and nonrare items on the basis of subject. In my opinion and experience this fusion greatly complicates the rare book function in any library of size, and it militates against the acceptance of that function by readers. If the rules of an institution are such that any book in the rare book division must be administered according to the regulations governing rare books, whether it is one or not, reader frustration will run high. On the other hand, if a double-standard operation is permissible, the rare book librarian will be forced to defend his rules in every borderline instance. Either way he will be bedeviled endlessly. Nevertheless, many librarians, for reasons that to them are equally valid, adhere to the view that a single service point for a well-defined subject area is preferable—that *Isis* and *Osiris,* for example, should be shelved in the same department that houses the rarities related to the history of science, with which so many of their articles deal.

REFUSAL OF GIFTS

Not infrequently a new acquisition is the signal for publicity, originating either with the institution or the donor, or both. This is invariably welcomed, because generosity begets generosity, and additional gifts may be expected to result. But sometimes these may seem to have little relevance to the institution's objectives, and indeed the librarian may find himself faced with the delicate problem of refusal. He would do well to be wary in this. If his judgment is faulty, he not only risks creating donor resentment—he may also miss a nonrecurring opportunity to acquire materials for which unforeseen usefulness may one day arise. If the issue is clear-cut, however, a little extra effort on the part of the librarian will preserve good will and friendly relations, because it is nearly always possible to recommend a repository where the gift will be useful and gladly received. In my own experience prospective donors are usually grateful for guidance in finding the right place for their donations; the librarian who is helpful is never forgotten.

The foregoing paragraphs have at times wandered willfully away from the subject of this chapter. The writer admits his innate inability to bypass paths that open before him; moreover, every phase of rare book librarianship commands his deepest interest. At the same time it is all too obvious to him that many of the problems which may develop during the assimilation of a new collection have eluded discussion here, largely because the variables involved in the nature of a collection on the one hand and the nature of a recipient library on the other make generalizations difficult.

For example, in special research libraries, as in those of the more typical historical societies, the fields are usually well defined, and the weeding of nonrelevant material tends to follow clear-cut lines, as do the practices related to the organization of new materials. The chief problems are those of policy, occasioned when desirable collections are offered which will, if accepted, extend the avowed areas of interest. Public libraries and those of colleges and universities, however, usually build toward universal or at any rate very broad coverage; they tend to welcome collections which represent subject areas new to them. Their problems, accordingly, stem from their own magnitude rather than from their delimitations.

REORGANIZATION FOR SPECIAL PURPOSES

In rare book libraries it is highly desirable to have a certain flexibility in the arrangement of books on the shelves. The point has been made that subject alone seldom makes a book deserving of rare book treatment (erotica can be cited as a possible exception), and in consequence shelving strictly by subject may interfere with the requirements of proper rare book administration—requirements which, in fact, are not necessarily static in themselves. Inasmuch as shelf consultation of rare books by readers is not or *should not be* permitted, the rare book librarian is presumably free to make whatever changes in the shelving order of the books in his care which he feels will facilitate their preservation, augment their usefulness, or bring out particular facets that have not been or cannot be adequately emphasized in the cataloging.

The consideration of man-hours to one side, the rare book librarian should be able to effect such changes almost as a matter of course. He should be able to take advantage, without waiting for expensive and elaborate recataloging, of the many special listings that are constantly being produced, and to revise his shelving when such listings are revised. For example, a library specializing in American literature might find it useful to identify *and segregate* its early fiction on the basis provided by Wright's bibliographies. Wing, and Pollard and Redgrave, are excellent tools to facilitate the establishment of files of early English imprints, as are Evans for early American editions and Stillwell for incunabula.

Moreover, the librarian should be free to create, without reducing the efficiency of reader service, special groups of books requiring exceptional storage facilities, or meeting specialized needs: books valued at more than a thousand dollars, for example, or books with fore-edge paintings, those that must be laid flat, those containing important manuscript marginalia, those with chronograms or extra-illustrations or authors' presentation inscriptions, those for which facsimile reproductions are available. He may wish to create special files of forgeries, palimpsests, or illuminated books; he may wish to bring together his elephant folios, or miniature books, or books printed on vellum or bound in human skin. In short, he should be free to make, revise, or disband files of books on any basis whatever, to meet any need or exigency. If you are wondering why he would want to do such things, the answer is simply that he is a rare book librarian; it is in the nature of his job for him to be concerned with the esoteric and exceptional articles in his care as well as with the routine materials.

If his collection is small enough (not exceeding, say, 50,000 volumes), he may be able to keep within the scope of a one-man operation; he will know his books so well that the location of any single item is no problem to him. But this is a dangerous arrangement at best, the frailties of human nature being what they are, and in connection with large rare book libraries it is downright impossible—not only because of the difficulty of remembering details of many books, but also because other staff members of varying degrees of knowledgeability will be involved.

In certain rare book libraries, among which are those that began their existence as such and not as parts of larger, more general collections, formal subject classification systems are not used. Instead, some method of book location which is not part of the cataloging process is employed, and this sometimes consists of a finding record based on serial numbers. Matching numbers occur on the catalog cards and in the books; readers are instructed to include these numbers when filling out call slips. There is a corresponding file of numbered cards in the rare book stack, and on these cards the locations of the relevant books are noted. Changing the position of a volume on the shelves is, therefore, simply a matter of local record-keeping—and this, of course, permits the high degree of flexibility which is so desirable in rare book libraries. Although the method necessarily adds one full step to the stack attendant's work (he must first go to the location card before he can be certain of the whereabouts of a particular book), it is a step which may save many other steps.

Most rare book libraries, however, being subsequently formed departments or divisions of larger institutions (almost always the case with college, university, and public library rare book sections), have inherited the parental subject classification systems. The fact that a given volume is in the rare book collection rather than in the general library is usually indicated by some symbol or prefix to the regular classification number, and the arrangement of the books on the rare book shelves thus becomes a microcosm of the main library. Hardly any rare book librarian will agree that this is a good method, but the evolutionary processes by which rare book sections are formed in large general libraries are such that the appointment of a librarian is all too frequently the last phase. When the librarian reaches the scene he finds himself, more often than not, committed to an entrenched system; to change it substantially would set in motion a process amounting almost to complete recataloging. From a budgetary standpoint such a prospect is not to be lightly viewed, and in most instances the librarian resignedly accepts the situation, though he may be heard to mutter Omar's ninety-ninth quatrain with disquieting iteration.

Fortunately there are various ways of making-do. The most common device is the familiar dummy. This, shelved in the normal classification position, bears information showing the special location of the book in question. Inherent in the method, of course, is the fact that the stack attendant must go to two places, possibly at some distance from each other, before he obtains the needed volume. The method, nevertheless, has the advantage of being easily installed and reasonably dependable.

The writer, in his own institution, is laying the groundwork for another method, which has the merit of combining the standard subject classification system with the location-card device. It is simple in essence, and may very well already be in use in other rare book libraries. The key to the method is the provision of a special catalog of the rare books, arranged by classification numbers and installed in an advantageous place inside the rare book stack. All current recataloging and new cataloging of rare materials make provision for this file, which we call the "stack list." When eventually—we are a long way from completion—we have such cards for all of our books, we will be in a position to use the stack list as a location record. Irregularities of shelving will be noted in pencil on these cards, and the first step in the stack attendant's work of withdrawing books for readers will be to consult the location index. At the same time he has within easy reach, for use when books have been misplaced, all the information that the official catalog can supply.

Turning from the theoretical whys and hows of reorganization, we may now give some attention to their practical application. The librarian, faced with the necessity of reorganizing an existing collection, must meet and find answers for a variety of basic problems. The writer hopes that he will be forgiven for citing chapter and verse from his own experience; he dares to do so only because of his certainty that his situation is not unique—that it is, in fact, duplicated in many places where rare book departments of larger institutions have been set up without taking all of the factors into account.

My own library has been undertaking a reappraisal of its rare book facilities for a number of years. Our rare book department is not new, having been established in 1931, but its realignment into a Special Collections Division is a postwar development, by which a number of unit collections, nonrare as well as rare, have been brought together under a single administration. It was soon found that subjecting rare and ordinary works to the same use restrictions dealt overharshly with readers, especially when the ordinary books were not duplicated in the general files. It was obvious that double standards were not workable at a single service point—that distinctions between books, even when reading room attendants could be trained to make them, were to a material degree unintelligible to much of our clientele. Our reader relations were in serious danger of deterioration.

Accordingly, we have now entered a phase of discontinuing full-coverage subject groups in our Special Collections Division, and of relegating nonrare works to the general files when this course is not forbidden by conditions of gift or bequest. This has, of course, involved us in a root-and-branch reorganization process. The first collection to be given this treatment was a large file concerned with the history of economics, numbering some 38,000 volumes, which had been purchased in two lots in 1929 and 1942. This collection had not been officially cataloged, reader access to it being by means of the former owner's own handwritten cards; weeding nonrare working texts from it was, therefore, merely a matter of decision. Once the segregation was made, the cataloging proceeded apace: the rare and early volumes for Special Collections, the later works for the business or general libraries. No problem.

Other unit collections have since been given similar handling; in some cases, either partially or wholly cataloged groups were involved. One of these offered such a variety of special considerations that its story may be repeated in some detail.

For many years my institution had painstakingly developed a so-called Book Arts Collection, a full-coverage subject group comprising both exemplars of and works about all phases of printing and allied crafts. This collection numbered some 15,000 volumes and was officially classed as a rare book collection, although it included a substantial content of working texts and other nonrare materials. In 1942 a large *en bloc* purchase of similar materials was made, and this added another 17,500 books, among which was, of course, extensive duplication. The new acquisition, however, greatly changed the complexion of our holdings; what had been a collection designed merely to support courses of study in the Library School now became of research depth. The problem of how to go about amalgamating the two parts into a coherent whole (they contained different areas of emphasis) was not a simple one.

One decision provided the key to the entire situation, and once it was made, all other parts of the process fell into place. It was decided to have *two* collections: one a working group consisting of books that could be circulated or placed on reserve lists to cover course requirements, and the other made up of noncirculating exemplars and rarities. This is the structure of the present arrangement. The Book Arts Collection is (or will be when the recataloging work is completed) a concentration of rare books and exemplars from both the preexistent Book Arts Collection and the new acquisition; the Graphic Arts Collection will consist of all working texts and most periodicals.

As recataloging has proceeded, we have found that many items in both collections actually have either little worth or small relevance to the central theme; such items are being removed. We are, in other words, taking this opportunity to streamline the files, relegating to other parts of the library system those works which have primary usefulness elsewhere, and discarding altogether those which seem to be without usefulness of any kind.

One point in connection with this arrangement needs underscoring. If we had been content just to catalog all books in the new collection as *rare* books and to leave the others as they were, there would have been no problems to surmount—except, of course, that our files would have been woefully cluttered with useless and extraneous items, and we would have been endlessly pestered by readers rightfully questioning the integrity of our rare book collection. It was the decision to place in the circulating collection all books that *should* be allowed to circulate, retaining in the rare book section only those that should *not* circulate, that represents the true gain of the whole expensive process. And this, I think, is the key to the matter.

The content of rare book sections of larger libraries should consist only of rare books (if donor restrictions prevent this, the nonrare items should be duplicated on the open shelves); and the arrangement of materials within the rare book section should be flexible, efficient, and safe. Once these simple requirements are met, no reasonable reader will concern himself with the machinations of the librarian. When he requests what he knows or can have demonstrated to him to be a rare book, he cannot possibly care whether the librarian has arranged his materials by subject, shape, size, color of binding, or pure whimsey—provided that his request is honored quickly and efficiently. What goes on in the stack in the way of special methods of preservation, of satisfying the ego of the librarian, or for the delectation of occasional visitors is of no direct concern to the reader.

Chapter V

Processing Rare Materials

GEORGIA HAUGH

This section is written, frankly, with the novice in mind and, further, with small reliance on innate carefulness in human nature. Both experienced librarians and those who shy away from detail may question the need for the following minute admonitions and directives, but good care of books cannot be taken for granted. Library personnel as well as readers need reminders of the special nature of rare books.

Once a book has been termed a rarity by its owner—individual or institution—the question as to its treatment arises. Is it untouchable, or is it expendable in the same degree as other books? The answer lies somewhere in between, depending on the degree of rarity and on the library. General theories as well as actual practices may differ in application from library to library.

Undoubtedly, if a book is to be preserved, it will need safeguarding not only from theft but also from careless use. A major reason for such concern lies in the high initial cost and the difficulty or utter impossibility of replacement. For the many reasons already presented in previous papers, the book is not expendable. From the moment the book is received, it is considered as a permanent acquisition. Except in unusual circumstances it is not likely to be discarded or replaced by an equally good copy.

A second reason for special consideration stems from appreciation of the inherent character of an old book. For example, it was the practice formerly to replace an ordinary-looking cover with a new one, richly fashioned. But in collecting circles today there is a strong feeling that a rarity should be preserved, if at all possible, in its original condition, particularly in the quality of its binding. For that reason, even a deteriorated binding, if presumed to be contemporary, will be kept intact and the volume made presentable for the shelves by means of a protective case. Aside from this avowedly sentimental affection for the genuine, there is a practical reason for clinging to the original. Though fine new bindings are a delight to behold, they do obscure the

51

history of the book. The first binding might well be a primary point in scholarly research on a particular edition of a book, or even a certain copy.

As a rule, a rare book is reduced in value by alteration of its original state. While libraries will not be auctioning off their books in the foreseeable future, and obligations to heirs may seem nebulous except to the private collector, there still remains the responsibility not to reduce the value of an acquisition by careless or thoughtless attrition.

One more reason exists for preserving a book from disfigurement. Ideally, the atmosphere of the rare book room should be one of serenity and elegance, with fine appointments enriched by rows of handsome books. The books should have an aura of authenticity. The original and the true are here; the room and the books should so pronounce.

CAVEATS

Despite the various arguments for respectful handling of rare books, the fact remains that they must be subject to various techniques in processing just as are other materials in any well-organized library. A basic rule to follow is this—avoid exposing the book to anything which might provide an opportunity for injury. It is, of course, impossible to point out all the pitfalls for the unwary, or to offer all possible solutions. A compendium of common-sense practices follows.

Unwrapping

Awareness of specialty begins with the advent of the book into the building. Even an operation so prosaic as unwrapping must proceed most carefully. The beginner will notice that books received from antiquarian dealers are incased first of all in several folds of soft paper to prevent rubbing of the leather, next by heavier paper or perhaps waterproofing paper, and finally by stiff, corrugated cardboard. Despite these layers of protective padding, care must be exercised that the opening instrument does not penetrate through to a precious binding. Wrenching or ripping coverings, so habitual in common practice, must be curbed. (The same meticulous care should be taken in wrapping rare books that are sent from the library.)

After the package is opened, fragile items should be given interim protection. An unbound pamphlet can be placed in an envelope; a book with loose covers in a cardboard box. Covers of powdery leather should be wrapped in a temporary paper jacket, lest they leave a brownish residue on anything that comes in contact with them.

Checking In

The book is often forwarded to the staff member delegated to check it in before cataloging, usually a member of the order department. This individual must be impressed with the need for special precautions.

In a large library system, he may very well be uninformed about rarities; therefore, his job training should include instructions in their exceptional care. Normally, he will be alerted by specifications on the order card. It will then be his responsibility to insert a conspicuous marker in the book to make clear its destination.

Diligence at the point of entrance is important to assure favored treatment for rare items throughout the subsequent stages of processing. Otherwise, if the book passes by this key point unnoticed, it will be incorrectly routed and will suffer mutilation by embossing or perforating or by ink stamps, not to mention improper classification.

Cautions

To begin with, the normal habit of carrying an armload of volumes should be discouraged because of the extreme fragility of many rarities. Neither should they be stacked. An accident can loosen bindings and even dislodge them, as well as mangle pages. Sometimes, ironically enough, weak hinges of an old book, adequate enough for several years of occasional reader use, are worn through by the repeated openings during processing.

At no time should a book be left standing on its fore edge with leaves hanging down, because this pulls against the stitching. Whenever a book in use is to be left lying open, a velvet shot bag or glass plate of appropriate weight and size should be placed carefully across the leaves.

Only a slip of paper should be used as a bookmark, never a pencil or a ruler, and certainly the open book must not be placed face down. Leaves should be turned carefully and slowly with a light touch and by the outer edge when possible. In some departments, a rubber-tipped pencil or rubber finger protector is specified when collating. Wrinkled pages and dog-eared corners should be carefully smoothed out.

Obviously, extraneous substances like ink, food, water, and ashes are to be kept away from rarities. Mending with plastic tape is not recommended. In time, most varieties of this otherwise useful product will pull away, leaving a residue which even an expert finds virtually impossible to remove. Some rarities have lost most of their value because of this type of clumsy repair. Rubber bands ought not to be used to hold books open, either during cataloging or in an exhibit. If paper clips must be used for any reason, the leaf of the book should be protected by a fold of heavy paper stock or thin cardboard. The cataloger should remember that prolonged exposure in sunlight will bleach paper and fade bindings just as surely in the cataloging room as on the regular shelves, where every effort is made to keep strong light from the books.

Occasionally, it will be necessary to tie a cord around a book or a periodical. For this purpose, twilled tape or soft twine may be used, but binder's twine, which is often found in shipping rooms, should not be resorted to because it contains an oily preservative powerful enough to soak through many pages.

Many of these cautions apply also to nonbook materials such as maps, broadsides, newspapers, and manuscripts. In addition, their special format creates another hazard. Because of their size and flexibility, they often come to the library already folded. In time these creases will break through if they have not already done so. The items should be opened out flat, and, if necessary, oversize folders or boxes made for them. Sheet maps should be mounted in sections on a cloth background.

Opening Pages

In many libraries, there are strict injunctions against opening the pages of a rarity. For the uninitated it might be well to define "unopened" and "uncut"—a distinction fastidiously observed in antiquarian parlance and necessary for all curators to understand. "An unopened book is one whose untrimmed edges have not been opened by hand, as with a paper knife." "Uncut edges: Descriptive of a book whose leaves are untrimmed by machinery."[1] One of the refinements of the rare book world is the tribute paid an unopened copy because of its seeming freshness from the press of a century or more ago.

However, the terminology useful to rare book dealers and their patrons is not always the most useful to the working librarian. He must recognize a point where precision becomes preciosity. If the practical curator wants to make sure that an apprentice or reader does not open pages, he had better give specific instructions stating: "Do not *cut* the pages open with a letter opener (or paper knife)." In practice, the decision to open a rarity can be postponed until the time when it seems necessary to do so for reading purposes. Secondary works are ordinarily opened without hesitation. When leaves are opened, a bona fide letter opener with dull edge, or a bone folder, is more suitable than a sharp knife or a razor blade.

The same stipulation applies to uncut copies. The librarian should not take it upon himself to trim off ragged edges or to pare down a leaf that is larger than the others. Irregularities are inherent features. In fact, the strongest indictment against rebinding a volume lies in the heedless shearing of precious margins. Occasionally, a rebound book will reveal a turned-back, folded corner. Smoothed out, it serves as a tangible reminder of a once wider margin, but because of its awkward appearance, some curators may decide to trim it on less-important books.

---

[1] *The Bookman's Glossary* (4th ed., rev. and enl. by Mary C. Turner; New York: Bowker, 1961), p.169-70.

Collating

Brief mention should be made of collating, an essential phase of processing in rare book libraries. Stated sketchily, collating is leafing through the book page by page, signature by signature, checking for completeness, misnumbering, imperfections, and the inclusion and position of plates and maps, normally in comparison with another known copy.[2] This scrutiny is important to determine whether an acquisition is complete and in good condition after years of existence, and to make certain that an imperfect copy is not cataloged as perfect (and purchased as such).

Insertions

During this examination, unsolicited personal souvenirs may turn up: clippings, leaves (arboreal, that is!), locks of hair, notes, and letters. All of these are to be removed promptly—they may already have caused stains—and some of these mementos, such as the botanical specimens, will be discarded immediately without further thought. However, anything of association value is usually saved and placed with the book or elsewhere. A private collector may wish to place all important association items inside the front cover. Libraries may follow this practice, too, but eventually will find it annoying to cope with slips falling out whenever the book is opened. Furthermore, there is danger of damaging the binding by distention, or of staining nearby leaves with paper of inferior quality. A better solution would be to keep a file of related material in folders elsewhere, with a note in the book or on the catalog card referring to the item and its location. When the book is kept in a box case, such miscellaneous pieces may be placed in an envelope in the same container, provided proper attention is given not to crowd or damage the item.

Clippings may have been pasted in a book; if not, libraries might treat them as described above or, under certain conditions, dispose of them. However, if these have been firmly attached to the book or manuscript, they cannot always be removed.

Letters, whether by the author or a former owner, may be attached inside one of the covers by pasting them along the top or inner margin, or hinging them with transparent mending tape. However, even closely associated letters may likewise be transferred to a file designed to preserve them for possible reference. If there are assorted letters and notes, they may be transcribed to one neat sheet. Generally, though, conscientious curators will retain at least the important hands

---

[2]Further explanation, most meaningful to the processor, may be found in Harry Miller Lydenberg and John Archer, *The Care and Repair of Books* (4th ed., rev. by John Alden; New York: Bowker, 1960), p.11. A technical description of collating by signatures is given in R. B. McKerrow, *An Introduction to Bibliography for Literary Students* (Oxford: Clarendon Pr., 1927), p.73 ff.

in the original, often adding a transcription on more durable paper. In
this connection, it should be noted that paper placed in a rarity should
be of acid-free content to prevent staining and also to ensure permanence of the note. This kind of rag paper may be obtained from whole-
sale dealers carrying fine papers.

Book Jackets

Book jackets are usually saved either on the book or in a special
file, because they often contain biographical information and for some
collectors they are valuable attributes to the mint condition of the book.
Jackets kept on the book are not pasted on, as is the practice in libraries circulating books.

Photoduplication

Thoughtful curators are well aware of still another source of danger
to their charges in this age of praiseworthy service through microfilm-
ing and photostating. Even under the best of circumstances, filling such
a request imposes additional handling of the item. In photographing, the
pressure of flattening a book under glass, page by page, can be injuri-
ous (even though performed by conscientious operators), especially to
a book tightly bound or one with a paper back. Often the work must be
done outside the library building, which may be reason enough to make
the curator consider each request separately after examining the material which is needed by the photographic department.

FIATS

Confronted by these caveats and apprehensive that any handling of a
rare book or manuscript is taboo, the staff member learns that new
rare acquisitions are, after all, not delivered direct from the order
department to the shelves completely unmarked. They are brought
under control by some of the devices approved throughout the library
world. Bookplates are affixed, cataloging marks are inscribed, and
shelving aids are inserted. Ordinarily, book pockets and date due slips
are not appended since there is little or no circulation of a rare book
collection.

Nearly every library, regardless of kind or size, applies markings
of some kind to its collections: call numbers, designation of ownership,
as well as various symbols relating to ordering, accessioning, and
cataloging. The rare book library diverges from other libraries in the
amount and the kind of markings used. For example, many large libraries today, in the interests of economy and security, have replaced
the time-consuming bookplate by a book stamp applied prominently to
the fore edge of a book. Rare books should not be so branded. (Even
though there is a kind of historical precedent for this! First instances
of outside titles occurred on the fore edge because the book was shelved

horizontally with the fore edge showing.) The general rules are: the less tampering the better and anything superimposed on the book should be tastefully applied. One inviolable rule, however, is that nothing should be written on the title page.

The ideal practices may not always obtain, of course, since each library will formulate regulations according to its own requirements. For instance, the Library of Congress in recent years has found it necessary for reasons of security to stamp identification directly on the text of a manuscript. For special reasons other owners have adopted a similar practice.

Ownership Identification—Bookplates

Theoretically, to maintain the original state of the book, not even bookplates should be added, and a few libraries adhere to that strict policy. For practical reasons, however, most libraries do add plates. As a matter of fact, many rarities already contain bookplates of a former owner, and these should be invariably retained. Ownership by a noted collector or a famous person is highly prized by most librarians, and any evidence of provenance should by no means be removed from a book.

Before taking up the mechanics of inserting the bookplate, a few suggestions about the plate itself might be helpful for the new curator confronted with a decision in selecting one. Upon investigation, he will find that plates vary infinitely in size and appearance since they are an intimate expression of the owner's taste. Ordinarily, a plate is preferable to an inked stamp because of its refinement and possibilities for effective design. The plate should be big enough to contain sufficient information but not so large as to overpower the page. Connoisseurs with a keen eye for proportion might like to own several plates—either of the same design or a variant—in three sizes for small, medium, and large books. However, sometimes the cost of design and engraving precludes such indulgence, and the same *ex libris* is used for all sizes. If, occasionally, the plate is too large for the available space, the margins of the plates may be trimmed down by hand, but this practice is frowned upon by some curators.

Plates may be engraved on metal or wood, and printed by any one of the three printing processes; but regardless of the method used, careful thought should be given to appearance. The design should be restrained, yet interesting. Ungummed paper of good quality is recommended, although leather is occasionally used, even though there is often evidence of staining (or setoff) on the contiguous pages.

Sometimes the curator may rely on one plate design only, but occasionally he will order special ones to be used in books acquired as gifts or from gift funds. For miscellaneous small donations, a simple gift plate may be sufficient, so that information about donor and date of acquisition may be added. This gift plate may be identical to the general plate in all respects, or it may be an entirely new design. Typical phrases preceding the donor's name are: "Gift of," "Presented by," "From the Estate of," "In Memory of." But for a sizable bequest, a special plate may be in order, in which case the benefactor may be consulted about his preferences. Occasionally, the library might consider including its name as well as that of the donor in order to obviate pasting in two plates, although there are reasons for not recommending this practice as unalterable.

Even the simple matter of where to place the bookplate calls for some thought. The usual position is inside the front cover on the pasted-down half of the lining paper: centered, or in the upper left corner, or in the center near the top edge. A troublesome problem arises when the preferential areas have already been used by earlier owners, or when there are inscriptions on the lining papers. Libraries have found various means of solving this problem. If the plates are small enough, a new one may be placed neatly in any free area, making sure that an aesthetic balance is preserved.

However, an added plate may crowd the area and it would be better then to use the inside of the back cover where there is usually a clear surface for centering. If all logical places are occupied in both the front and the back covers, the plate may be tipped in lightly on the flyleaf or endpaper. Full pasting of a plate on a single endsheet is not recommended as it will wrinkle the paper. Ordinarily, a plate is not tipped in over another one, and it should never be pasted on top of another plate.

A plate already in the book should not be removed, except in unusual circumstances; at best it is a delicate operation and not to be undertaken lightly. Old plates should be left in books for many of the same reasons that have been given for preserving original bindings. Nor should a plate be transferred from one book to another, even though the duplicate copy appears to be superior in other respects. The provenance of either copy might be important in future research, and the sin of transfer unforgivable if there are marginalia identified with the bookplate. It is far better to keep both copies of the book when there is any reason for preserving distinguished provenance.

Sometimes the lining papers are illustrated, and most perceptive librarians prefer not to place an *ex libris* over any part of such endpapers. Some curators do not hesitate to plate over an illustrative map or plan when it is duplicated at front and back of the book, though others may prefer to tip in the plate in the back at the top edge. However, if the two maps are different and of any possible reference value to the reader, neither should be obscured. The plate may then be tipped in on the reverse side of the free endpaper.

The process of bookplating is not a simple routine. Frequently, it is a task turned over to new assistants, and even the most experienced worker can fail to understand deviations in respect to the kind of plate used and its unusual placement. Plates may easily be pasted in undesignated areas. Constant vigilance is required to ensure that directions are followed to the letter, particularly in regard to special plates which

may be used only infrequently. It is often wise for the individual responsible for the plate selection to indicate where the plate should be
put.

Accession Numbers

In addition to bookplates, other means of identification are used—
among them, the accession number. The use of accession numbers is
not so prevalent today as formerly, though in rare book libraries some
librarians still find it extremely useful to accession their collections.
Aside from the specific number assigned to each book, the accession
record provides a convenient means for determining the order of receipt of titles throughout the year. The accession number may be entered with pencil (or even ink) in a small but readable form in an in-
conspicuous place, for example, at the upper right-hand corner of the
inside of the back cover. A perforated stamp should never be used, or
even an inked stamp, unless the library has decided upon this as a
security measure.

Some libraries use so-called secret marks at certain pages known
only to them. One famous method of marking was that used by Thomas
Jefferson, who minutely inscribed a "T" immediately in front of the
printed signature "I" (i.e., "J") and a "J" after "T." Naturally, many
other systems have been used, but these are not generally known. The
chief function of an ownership mark is to discourage theft, and to make
identification positive upon recovery after a theft. Another method of
identification is to provide a careful description of the physical aspects
of the book in the permanent records of the library, usually on the catalog card. Such details should include the style and color of binding, as
well as inscriptions and bookplates, or any particular features requiring annotation.

Processing

Besides bookplates and ownership marks, various bits of data useful to the staff may be added to the book. Some or all of these may be
furnished: the price, date acquired, and sources; collation note; classification; cataloging entry; and bibliographical references. In many
libraries the first group, relating to ordering, is not considered essential, particularly when an accession number has been assigned. The
number serves as a reference to these facts in the accession record.

The purist may want to refrain from practicing certain library
science techniques, but most curators find, as the collection grows,
that it is convenient and even necessary to have pertinent data close at
hand. One way to circumvent writing in the book itself is to type all
this information on a slip to be laid in or tipped in the back of the book.
Any inscriptions made in the books should be in pencil, not ink, and
written neatly and in an unintrusive position.

Call Numbers

There is no general agreement about which position is best for writing the call number on or in the book.[3] It is usually placed near the upper corner of the selected area, frequently inside the front or the back cover. Call numbers may be found also on the flyleaf, the page following the title page, near the bookplate, and on the verso of the title page. Many authorities recommend the position inside the back cover but allow for certain exceptions. If the call number cannot be written clearly on an endpaper because of the color or condition of the lining paper, it may be written on the last blank leaf. For an unbound item which is laid in a slipcase, it may be permissible to write the number in pencil at the bottom of the last printed leaf, if no final blank leaf is in the book.

Entry Notation

The customary library practice of indicating the cataloging entry on the title page by placing three dots under the key word, or by under-scoring it or writing it out in full, is not recommended by most cura-tors for rare books. Such annotations detract from the original state of the item whenever a title page is reproduced or exhibited. But if the volume has the signature of Napoleon or Washington already written there, leave it, as it enhances the value of the book.

This is not to say that the very useful notation of the entry should be eliminated, but that it should be added in a less conspicuous place than on the title page. A logical place might be inside the back cover where it can be written near the call number. Some catalogers have elected to write on the blank page opposite the title page, but this prac-tice is not recommended by most curators.

Collation Note

A note of collation may be written near the cataloging entry. Usu-ally the note is brief: "Collated" or "Collated perfect" with the date. Any deficiencies, if not too numerous, might be added, such as "Plate at p. 9 lacking." It is useful to have this information in the book when comparing two copies or to give an immediate answer to a reader in-quiry. When the imperfections are too complicated to be neatly listed in the book, then it is better to refer to the catalog card for a full des-cription or to type them on a slip that can be laid in the book.

So much for pencil work by the librarian. What about marks al-ready in the book? Since previous bookplates are left in, should addi-tional marks also be retained for the sake of association? Unquestion-ably, nonsense scribbling and doodling might safely be erased unless

---

[3]Margaret Mann, *Introduction to Cataloging and the Classification of Books* (2d ed.; Chicago: American Library Association, 1943), p.86.

there is good reason to believe that they were made by famous persons. Clearly, names and annotations in manuscript by former owners, or the author, should be saved as part of the history of the book, and most rare book libraries make a card for each signature for their special provenance file.

Book dealers frequently leave evidence of their descriptions in the volumes. They often write their coded price inside the covers, and sometimes bibliographical or descriptive notes for their own convenience. Even the title page may have been used for that purpose. Certain librarians may feel the urge to erase such marks. When markings occur elsewhere in the book, they are usually left untouched unless they detract from the appearance of the book. Inscriptions written by bibliographers of certain antiquarian book firms oftentimes provide association interest and may be of historical value.

Spine Labels and Shelving Aids

A noticeable feature of most rare book libraries is the absence of call numbers on the spines of the books. In order to maintain a neat appearance of the collection, as well as to aid in preserving the intrinsic value of each book, the decision to forego the convenience of a label or inked number is deliberate in many rare book collections. This practice, however, need not extend to the reference collections, although in some rare book libraries even the reference collections are not labeled on the backs of the books.

On the other hand, efficiency is not to be entirely disregarded. As the collection grows and staff members come and go, it may be advantageous to facilitate shelving and searching. Certain devices have been introduced which help the user to locate a volume by some means other than opening a book to the call number.

A common method is to insert a slip inside the back cover which will extend above the top of the book. This procedure may be objectionable in appearance to some librarians. Another method used by some librarians is to insert a slip at the rear of the book, i.e., extending from the fore edge, which is of course at the back when shelved. This position, admittedly, is of no help in searching out a certain book, but is of some assistance in verifying a book once it is pulled out from the shelf and is, of course, invaluable in reshelving. This slip may be placed loose in the book, usually in the back, or attached to an endpaper by the use of a slit. Once more it should be said that all slips coming in contact with the book should be made from acid-free paper. At some libraries, when a protective case is made, the binder provides an index tab on the back edge with the call number on it.

One means of making the classification number easily visible without marring the exterior of the book is to place the items in box cases which carry the call numbers gilded on the spine. Many curators, however, reject the idea of shelf after shelf of boxed books in a library where original leather or vellum bindings usually contribute to the general appearance of a fine collection.

The binder's title on the spine should be more helpful in arranging books than it usually is. Unfortunately, if there is one at all, it is often misleading if not thoroughly incorrect; and many times it does not include the date of imprint. For ease in finding a book the date is very important if a chronological classification scheme is used. The other data should reproduce, in shortened form, the cataloging entry and wording of the title as given on the title page. Some curators specify all of these points whenever a slipcase is ordered or a book is rebound. At least one library orders the location number stamped on the spine of the book if it is rebound in a modern binding.

For books not being rebound or boxed, corrections may be made on the spine by having the binder apply a new leather label over the old, or by stamping a date at the base of the spine. Certain rarities should not be subject to these emendations, but since many of the most valuable books are placed in boxes for protection from dust and light, the outer case may be titled correctly without altering the binding of the book.

The same reservation applies to signs on the shelves, for conspicuous labeling is not considered *comme il faut* in certain exhibition areas. Some location guides, however, may be desirable. One library places in each bookcase a dummy volume bound in half leather, with the information stamped in gold on the spine.

For books housed in closed stacks, the problems are not so serious. Some devices that have been suggested for books in display areas could be utilized to avoid using labels on the rarities, but protruding call numbers, slips, and shelf labels might be acceptable in closed stacks.

Incidentally, the effect of classification on shelving should be pointed out here as one of the considerations in the important and far-reaching choice of a classification scheme. When call numbers are not visible on the books, a simple scheme will be easier to use than a complicated one. An arrangement by subject with numerous categories is the most awkward of all, and in a library where browsing is not permitted, the convenience to the staff in regard to classification may be given first consideration.

When a library does not have labels on the spines of the volumes as an aid in locating books, it is usually wise to adopt a simple scheme, such as an arrangement by author, date of imprint, or accession number. All of these are obvious and readily understood from the call number inside the book, from a slip laid in it, or from a binder's title. There are libraries where various factors, such as use or size of collection, make close classification wise. If this is the case, from the viewpoint of shelving it would seem almost mandatory to place the call number on the outside of the book or at least to insert slips, though even these are only substitutes for a label on the spine. After all, if we return to the original premise that a rare book is not to be defaced, we may find it necessary to make certain compromises.

Shelving

It should be kept in mind that books are vulnerable to wear over the years through perils encountered in shelving. Books should stand next to each other in firm support—not too tightly, not too relaxed. If left tipping over in a slanted position, they become warped. Leather bindings are easily scratched and should not be crowded too close to either end of the shelves, particularly those which have metal adjustable strips. A buffer piece of cardboard may be interposed if necessary. Books with clasps may be boxed or protected with a piece of cardboard made to fit around the inside edge and sides so that it does not show on the shelves, or small patches of leather or cloth may be placed over the abrasive clasp.

Large folios should lie flat; if a large book cannot be shelved naturally but must be placed on edge, some libraries say that it should rest on the spine rather than on the fore edge to avoid straining the stitched binding; others say the opposite, to prevent dust from settling on the fore edges of the volumes. A better solution is to have a separate section for oversize books, designated by an appropriate sign in the call number, or perhaps by a dummy in the expected location referring to the special section.

When books are shifted, they ought to be lifted rather than pushed like blocks along the shelves. Incidentally, those who advocate shelving by size in accession order have a strong argument here. Wear and tear on books are inevitable whenever the ceaseless interfiling and shifting of a classified arrangement are used, but this is not the case when each new book is added according to accession numbers in particular size groups.

Most important of all, no book, least of all a rare book, should be pulled from the shelves by the top of the spine, as this often damages the headcap. The book should be withdrawn carefully by grasping the spine, first pushing back the adjacent books if necessary. When books are shelved too tightly for this, it will be necessary to reach over the book and apply pressure from behind the book.

It should be emphasized that ideally books are not shelved until they are in good condition. This means that all repairs are completed, and protective cases provided for those books that are not to be rebound. Leather bindings, if dry, should be properly treated with leather dressing. If, for reasons of expediency, books must be shelved before preparation processes are finished, temporary boxes may be utilized.

Instructions to Readers

Finally, the staff must instruct readers in their responsibility for careful handling of rare materials. In particular, readers should heed the caution against the use of ink, placing of markers in books, laying the books face down, opening of pages by cutting, writing in books, and heavy-handed turning of pages. Special rarities are subject to even greater care. Most of these regulations for use may be conveyed by a printed list presented to each reader at the time when he is registered as a qualified user. [4]

Although the foregoing caveats may seem elementary and extremely cautionary, the experienced librarian knows that the uninitiated users of rare materials often are guilty of gross negligence and carelessness where handling of books is concerned. To ease the burden of training in this era of rapid staff turnover is reason enough for this detailed treatment. Perchance the veteran may even find himself yielding to human frailty in failing to follow some of the specific procedures required for the proper care of rarities.

[4]For a more detailed treatment of the reader and the book, see the writer's "Reader Policies in Rare Book Libraries," *Library Trends*, 5, no.4:467-75 (April 1957).

Chapter VI

Cataloging and Classification

JOHN E. ALDEN

That one of the principal objectives of the rare book collection is the physical preservation of materials which, in Randolph G. Adams' phrase, are not expendable need scarcely be questioned. To achieve this end it is necessary to segregate such materials and to impose restrictions upon their use. Such regulations, needless to say, on occasion arouse the indignation of scholars, who disclaim any barrier between book and reader. Without considering the merits of such indignation, it has always seemed to me that the best answer to this criticism is that, while the rare book librarian seems to withdraw with one hand, he is offering lavishly with the other, and any diminished use caused by limited access, or the like, is more than compensated for by the facilities offered the scholar by other means.

Of such means the foremost to my mind is the specialized cataloging which is essential to the rare book collection. Admittedly, there are those who see no reason why rare books should be given cataloging any different from that of a current trade book. But such individuals are missing a great opportunity to render a particular, not to say unique, service to the scholar—the opportunity to describe individual books analytically and to achieve significant patterns either by the correlation of these descriptions or, by means of classification, by the correlation of the books themselves.

What is this specialized cataloging called for in recording rare books, and how does it differ from ordinary cataloging? Or, in what way is ordinary cataloging inadequate for the needs of the rare book collection?

To answer these questions we must, first, recognize the revolution in descriptive cataloging which has taken place in American librarianship during the past twenty years or more, and particularly the simplifications which have been introduced. In the face of the proliferation of books, the cataloger has been forced to reconsider—courageously, it must be said—what is absolutely essential in the description of mass-

65

produced books, as they pour from the presses, in terms of their contemporary readers. (I recognize, admittedly, that by earlier standards *any* book seemed a mass-produced work, yet I believe I may be allowed this relative comparison.) The simplified cataloging currently provided by the Library of Congress and widely followed throughout the country is, in terms of the books usually described and the uses to which they are put, a commendable solution to the tremendous problem involved. In saying this I do not begrudge but, rather, applaud the steps taken to break the bottleneck created by earlier cataloging codes injudiciously applied.

The fact remains, however, that for rare books such simplified cataloging is not universally adequate, nor would the devisers of it claim that it is. Its inadequacies arise from a variety of reasons. Of these one is the fact that, while simplified cataloging does purport to distinguish between different combinations or styles of type, the methods of simplified cataloging, if adequate for distinguishing between books produced in our day, are not sufficient for early printed books where variations occur with greater frequency.

In the second place, there is, or should be, a difference in point of view between the cataloging of the generality of books and the cataloging of rare books. This can perhaps be best suggested in terms of the preoccupation of the cataloger of ordinary books with the text or the contents of the books. It is the responsibility of the cataloger to report what the books say textually. This is perfectly valid, and it is usually sufficient.

But there are books which are important for reasons beyond their contents. Behind the efforts of all who have attempted to define the phrase "rare books," there lies a recognition that some books are important as physical objects, apart from, or in addition to, their contents. Such books possess some value or quality, be it intellectual or emotional, to be found in no other embodiment of the same text. What these values may be can vary from book to book; they range from those of age, scarcity, beauty, commercial value, or associations with earlier owners or events to their place in a sequence of editions—all apart from the words, the actual text, which they contain that may be found elsewhere.

In the third place, the rare book collection has a particular contribution to make to an area of scholarship for which simplified cataloging makes little provision. This is the history of printing, and of the graphic arts in general. The needs and purposes of the bibliographer and the historian of typography should be constantly considered in the shaping of cataloging policy.

The cataloger of rare books is accordingly confronted with several facets of the book, and in portraying them the methods of simplified cataloging are likely to fail him. This is particularly true of the need for distinguishing variations in the text itself, or in the physical components of a book. The recognition of the need for making—and interpreting—such distinctions is, in fact, one of the remarkable phenomena

of the book world of our day. It is not just a matter of making certain
that one possesses the *first* edition (state, or issue) of a book for the
sake of primacy alone. The present century has seen the development
of a new concept of bibliography at the hands of men such as R. B. Mc-
Kerrow, Sir Walter Greg, and Fredson Bowers.

As a result we are increasingly aware that the physical character
of a book can have great significance for the textual critic—a significance hitherto underestimated. The vagaries which may be found in a
book with text composed by hand, the possible changes in the course of
passing through the press, the use of cancel leaves—in short, all the
conceivable idiosyncrasies of early printed books—are now recognized
as never before as possessing potential meaning in relation to textual
content. There has been created a palaeography for the book as well
as for the manuscript which has opened up new avenues of scholarship.

Such studies of the physical peculiarities to be found in books have
required of the scholar a new discipline. Its importance and fruitful-
ness—solving, as it does, many of the textual problems which have baf-
fled earlier scholars—have yet to be fully exploited, but having seen how
Fredson Bowers has won over his earlier critics, especially those in
England, I am certain that the future will amply justify our confidence
in his methods.

Is it, to be sure, the function of the librarian to take cognizance of
these developments in bibliography? Should they, on the contrary, be
left to the bibliographical specialist, the compiler of analytic or enu-
merative bibliographies, the textual critic? Is it not enough for the
cataloger of rare books to conform to normal cataloging, and to ignore
this new dimension of cataloging?

This has been done and can be done, no doubt, for justifiable reasons. But to do so is perhaps a counsel of despair. The more productive view is certainly that the "new bibliography" is the province not
only of the avowed bibliographer but also of the rare book cataloger,
who in the course of his day-to-day activity has occasion to contribute
to knowledge and to scholarship by his own discoveries or by making
possible discoveries at the hands of others. It is for this reason above
all, no doubt, that rare book cataloging should reflect an awareness and
understanding of the importance of a book as a physical object and as
an artifact with possible meaning beyond itself.

At the same time, such cataloging should be achieved as economically and as effectively as possible, making the most productive use of
the means available. Normally this means, in America, that we are
committed to the use of the dictionary catalog on cards—with the limitations and resources of each. And most of us find ourselves working
within the framework of a larger general collection, of either a public
or a university library, the needs of which must also be considered.

What use shall we make, then, of the card catalog? Libraries have
been known not to record their rare books in their public catalogs at
all, in order to avoid indiscriminate use. But the consequences of this
may be that even the discriminating may be unaware of the existence in

a library's collections of material available to him. Another expedient is to record rare book material only under the main entry, but this, again, is a high price to pay for preservation.

As far as the character of our cataloging is concerned, there is also a possible choice in the form we give to it. We can use the card catalog, and simplified cataloging, for its usual ends—to record content; and then create a separate specialized catalog for bibliographic purposes. This specialized catalog may be achieved by providing a special file giving fuller descriptions, and the like, not recorded on the catalog cards. An example of this is the sheet description often employed for incunabula. For the small collection of extremely complex books this may well be the wisest course. But to adopt it for larger and comparatively heterogeneous collections is perhaps to underestimate the potentialities and the adaptability of the card catalog, especially of the unit card which can easily and economically be duplicated in multiple copies. I, for one, continue to believe in the suitability of the card catalog for rare books.

As a matter of fact, perhaps the greatest difficulty in using the card catalog for rare book cataloging is less a technical than a human problem. Part of this may very well be the fault of the rare book cataloger. It is all to easy for those connected with rare books to arrogate to themselves something of the distinction of the books with which they deal. But the fact that rare book cataloging does make demands of a varied nature upon the cataloger is no excuse for being patronizing toward those whose responsibilities are not the same. Nor is it easy for the general cataloger to discover that the hard-learned disciplines of simplified cataloging do not exhaust the possibilities of what cataloging may be. Good will, humility, and tact are indeed essential for the rare book cataloger. Given these, the card catalog itself is adaptable enough to serve the objectives of both rare book cataloging and general cataloging.

Provided that the cards produced can be integrated and interfiled within the larger catalog, there need be no reason why the form and content of rare book descriptions should follow a rigid conformity to convention as such. The plea for consistency in descriptive cataloging has already been undermined by the changes in practice of the Library of Congress itself, and both simplified cataloging and earlier, more elaborate forms will be found in most of our card catalogs. Few people are seriously inconvenienced or confused by this, if they give it any thought at all. As a consequence, this argument cannot be used against the rare book cataloger who seeks to be allowed latitude in the contents of his cards in order to treat adequately the books he seeks to describe.

But what really constitutes rare book cataloging, or what may be called—not too mysteriously—bibliographical cataloging? As a guide we should keep in view particularly the means required for distinguishing the identity, the uniqueness, of an individual book in its many possible aspects. In all of this genuine humility is required. There may have been a time when a cataloger could believe that a book once

cataloged would remain so cataloged. Our increasing bibliographic sophistication leads us, however, to believe that much of our cataloging—
as far as rare books are concerned—is at best tentative.

Nor, quite frankly, has any technique of bibliographical description
as such ever succeeded in every possible case in differentiating between all variants. Not infrequently only actual confrontation of the
several copies will reveal the variations between different states or
even editions, as anyone who has worked with post-Restoration English
books will attest. We may also feel, with some justice, that with apparent duplicate copies before us we cannot afford—especially when the
book is not of major importance—to make a word-by-word comparison
in a detailed search for in press variants. However attractive this
task for the cataloger, it perhaps can be left for the analytical bibliographer.

No, the rare book catalog is not a bibliography, in the sense of providing the last word, within the framework chosen, of the books described. But in our rare book cataloging we can provide a stepping-
stone between the simple finding list and the exhaustive bibliography;
we can, in the course of describing what we possess in a significant
fashion, provide signposts and achieve a high bibliographical standard.

The media through which we can attempt our differentiations are
our transcriptions of the title page, our collations, and the notes which
we provide. Within these terms we can go far toward giving a picture
of a book which will reveal its character, its individuality. Not only,
for instance, will the transcription of the title and of the imprint reveal
much about the content of the book, but also many of its differences
from other combinations of type. How full and how literal the transcription should be must remain, in good part, a matter of judgment.
This does not mean, for the purposes of cataloging, that line endings
need be indicated, or capitalization reproduced within the limits of
even a typewriter. For the few fish caught by these nets, the time and
effort involved are unlikely to be justified. But if extreme methods of
transcription are to be avoided, so, I think, should some of the short-
cuts and abbreviations of standard cataloging. Many of them probably
owe much to the day when catalog cards were written by hand, and
every stroke of the pen eliminated was a saving. Such savings are less
essential in our day, and with rare books I think them unnecessary.

Another convention of standard and of simplified cataloging which
has little place in specialized cataloging is the use of stylizations for
the imprints: place, printer, publisher, and date. To give the imprint
in full as it appears on the title page strengthens the possibility of
distinguishing variants, and will also serve the historian of printing
and publishing who is using the cards. If a concession must be made
to those for whom Roman numerals present a difficulty, a translation
of the date into Arabic figures may be provided in brackets.

In the collation, as in the title and the imprint, simplified cataloging, recording as it does only numbered groups of pages, destroys another opportunity for establishing variations. Nor does it provide a

guide to the completeness of the copy at hand, which, with rare books, is a matter of importance. The practice of giving a detailed collation of the "ideal copy"—in the state in which it was sold by its original printer or publisher—is a proven one, permitting the cataloger to record imperfections. Admittedly, the convention which confines the collation to printed pages or leaves alone is inconsistent with the thesis that a book is a physical object to be considered in its fullest sense, in which blank leaves are part of the story. For unpaged books, or for those whose composition is bewildering, giving a collation by signatures as well will often be very helpful.

Beyond these means we have recourse to the notes which we may provide. Besides those appropriate to general cataloging there are several sorts which may be useful for rare books. In this category fall vignettes or borders on the title page, and printer's marks there or elsewhere in the volume; such notes become even more valuable when reference is given to catalogs of them such as R. B. McKerrow's *Printers' and Publishers' Devices*. So far as is practicable, mention of errors in paging will also prove valuable, and cancel leaves should be recorded. The presence of errata is also potentially significant and should always be noted.

The real problem in providing notes is unquestionably one of keeping a sense of proportion. There is a danger of zealous overelaboration —the provision of descriptive material which does not serve a useful or valid purpose. To say, for example, that an eighteenth-century book contains head- and tailpieces is not, I expect, going to add greatly to our knowledge. Nor are we trying to sell the book, and our annotations need not read like a bookseller's catalog. At the same time, we might well bear in mind in our annotations the desirability of indicating, when it is not self-evident, just why the book is considered a rare book. Often the very date will explain its treatment as one. The fact that a book may yet be proved not to be the first edition we honestly believe it to be need not intimidate us, or deter us from giving this as our reason for assigning it rare book status. Similarly we may well call attention in our notes to earlier ownership or associations of the copy at hand, and describe, within reasonable limits, bindings which are publisher's bindings or remarkable for their quality. On the other hand, an ordinary nineteenth-century Sangorski and Sutcliffe binding as such probably does not call for comment, whatever our personal fondness for morocco!

In all of this, quite obviously, there is no substitute for judgment and discrimination—an understanding, on one hand, of the book and bibliographical problems and, on the other, of the needs of scholars in a variety of fields. If any simplification for our descriptions is justified, it may well be found in the use of references to existing competent bibliographies, which identify the book at hand and obviate the need of fuller descriptions than those provided for nonrare book material. Still another expedient in providing information that need not complicate the catalog cards excessively is the use of the back of the main (author) card for recording it; here can be recorded profitably the source of the copy cataloged, bibliographical information utilized, the collation by signatures if not given on the face of the card, a description of the binding, and the like.

The perceptive person will recognize that, in essence, the above recommendations follow closely the *A.L.A. Catalog Rules, Author and Title Entries* (Preliminary American 2d ed., 1941), taking advantage of its permissive practices for rare and early books. For this no apology need be offered. Here are provided forms by which significant information can be purposefully conveyed. But these forms must be enlivened by the cataloger's own intelligence. However platitudinous the observation may be, the fact remains that the quality of rare book cataloging is dependent upon the cataloger. To meet his responsibilities the rare book cataloger should believe in the validity of the bibliographical approach to books, must be familiar with its principles and with the history and practice of printing, and must be cognizant of the work which has been done and is being done by bibliographers elsewhere.

In the list of attributes of a good rare book cataloger a high place must be given to a lively scepticism—a scepticism, above all, regarding whether or not the book really is what it purports to be. For the history of printing and of book collecting is, candidly, replete in deception! To perceive these deceptions is a function of the cataloger at once amusing and valuable. On the one hand, the cataloger should recognize, as such, books with false places or dates of publication on the basis of his familiarity with type, paper, format, and the like. On the other, the cataloger must be alert to recognize deceptive descriptions of items offered for sale as genuine, books with facsimile leaves, or sophisticated copies, whose scholarly significance is accordingly affected. The need for constant vigilance against deception, a lively suspiciousness, can scarcely be overstated. But such bibliographical detective work adds a bit of zest to the cataloger's work.

Having described a book, the rare book cataloger has not, of course, completed his task. In other words, what pattern should the cataloger give to these descriptions, aided by the card—duplicated as it can be in multiple copies? Frankly, the usefulness of many subject headings for early books may be questioned, partly because of the semantic inadequacy of standard subject terminology and partly because of the shift in the meanings of words and in the approaches of scholars to their material in the course of centuries. Whether or not the scholarship produced in America, where comprehensive subject cataloging is provided by libraries, surpasses that of Europe, where such subject cataloging is far less intensive, may also be questioned. But to abandon such subject cataloging is unlikely to find acceptance among library administrators, and the rare book cataloger may reasonably continue to provide subject entries within the forms provided by American library practice, whatever his misgivings about their usefulness.

More useful, no doubt, is the attention given to individuals. The history of the past is above all the history of human beings, and the

limitations of simplified cataloging upon analyzing and recording the
contributions of a variety of authors can validly be suspended for early
books. Similarly there is no reason why the rare book cataloger should
not provide cards, at least for his own catalog—using his unit card—for
illustrators and engravers, for illustrations, maps, and the like.

Whatever we chose to provide in terms of subject headings or of
entries for individuals, such material can be fitted into the framework
of the dictionary catalog. But, in addition, there are further patterns
which have proved to be fruitful, and these add substantially to the facilities of the rare book collection which has provided them. There is,
first of all, the chronological file of cards by year of publication for
the collection—a convenience to the scholar concerned with the historical development of a subject field. The imprint catalog, with cards
arranged by country subdivided by city and then by year, is of value to
the historian of printing especially. If it is less often used by the literary or social historian, this is perhaps because he has not yet become familiar with its advantages. Most rare book collections will
also wish to record the names of previous owners of their books in a
provenance file. Another useful file is one that records outstanding
bindings, by country and period, or by binder. The Houghton Library
at Harvard even maintains an informal file for the individuals to whom
books have been dedicated, although its usefulness has been challenged.

The debates over the relative merits of classification schemes for
the general collections find their reflection in those for rare books.
But here, again, the fact that a rare book is likely to be important for
reasons other than its subject matter applies and affects our approach
to its classification. Basically, one assigns call numbers to books in
order to locate them. What is too often forgotten is the fact that in
devising classification schemes we are attempting, really, to make
this purpose serve a further purpose, however valid it may be. With
rare books we have to ask what further purpose, or purposes, this shall
be. Shall it, indeed, be an analysis of knowledge or of the subject matter of books, or is there something else more important? What do we
need to do that is not done by our dictionary catalog or by the special
files or catalogs which we have also provided?

The library which arranges its books chronologically on its shelves
is indeed doing something worthwhile, but if it also has a chronological
card file among its catalogs, then it is certainly duplicating its efforts.
Much is to be said for keeping special gifts together as a unit, but accession records may already provide this information. Other libraries
may seek to organize their collections by national literatures, broken
down by century or half century, and then by author, as is done at the
Houghton Library—though not without exceptions, of which the typographical collection is an example. In the author approach to classification, one escapes the limitations imposed by a subject classification,
which also ignores the book as a physical object. But in all classification schemes there are disadvantages, and we are confronted with a
choice of evils. If, having considered a variety of possibilities, we

decide to accept a subject classification, we at least recognize that subject matter does play an important part in the writing of books. However much we may stress the book as an artifact in our descriptive cataloging, perhaps when we come to classification we can amend this emphasis.

Mention should be made of the advantage of a separate designation scheme for the rare book collection, whereby the call number shows quickly and clearly that the book is not part of the general collections. A distinct classification does permit this, or prefixing—as an example—Library of Congress classification numbers with an X.

If, in the foregoing, more emphasis has been placed on ends rather than on means in cataloging and classifying rare books, this is as it should be. That a revolution in American cataloging became necessary was due to the fact that catalogers too long had focused their attention upon how they should catalog, rather than considering what purpose cataloging served. If, in simplified cataloging, it appears at times that the baby has been thrown out with the bath, the rare book cataloger can at least take warning, lest he commit the same mistake or provoke an exaggerated adverse response. True, the rare book cataloger should be thoroughly familiar with the varying forms and levels of cataloging and classification, their merits and shortcomings. But he should be a bookman before he is a cataloger, a humanist before he is a technician. With these principles in mind he is more likely to provide cataloging which serves a more imaginative usefulness—a usefulness which will go far toward offsetting the inconveniences imposed by the needs of preservation.

That I have not given specific directions in these few pages whereby a qualified person could set forth to catalog and classify a rare book collection is all too obvious. Indeed, I should hesitate to undertake writing even an entire volume devoted to rare book cataloging, since the form such cataloging should take must above all respond, not to a code, but to the character and the purpose of the individual collection. The books themselves and not a preconceived notion of cataloging rules must shape the catalog of a specific library. In establishing practices to be followed for his collection, the rare book cataloger will be fortunate if he has had experience elsewhere—I am tempted to add, "particularly experience under Bill McCarthy of the Rosenbach Foundation"—but experience should not limit his imagination, the imagination to adapt himself to the collection at hand and to envisage how generously it may be made useful. For usefulness, above all, is the objective of rare book cataloging.

Chapter VII

Care, Maintenance, and Restoration

COLTON STORM

Rare book librarians are often appalled by the way readers, scholars, and other librarians handle books and manuscripts. Stories of razor blades, kippered herrings, and bacon rinds used as bookmarks are unfortunately true. It is also true that readers and scholars have mutilated books unmercifully by excisions, or with witty, profound, or vulgar marginal notes; it may not be true that librarians have done likewise, but the suspicion is strong that there are a few renegades who have shown somewhat less than respect for the properties placed in their charge. Sadly, this is true of some of our predecessors who became rare book librarians only because they had been unsatisfactory in every other department of the library.

Let us assume for convenience that today's rare book librarians are a superior race and that they have an unshakable respect for the book as an inviolable physical object. Let us assume further that a rare book librarian will never, under any circumstances or provocation, willingly cause any book in his care to change in appearance except for the better. His ideal will be always to secure and conserve materials as close to original condition as is humanly possible, expecting, naturally, few if any miracles in this far from perfect world. The rare book librarian will certainly think long and carefully before he makes any attempt to "better" the condition of any book. And he may even lay down his career to prevent anyone from willfully damaging a book.

In order to protect or conserve rare books, the rare book librarian ("curator" is probably a better word than the unwieldy phrase "rare book librarian") ought to have some good idea of how to handle rare books himself. Not all curators do, but they are learning. It is rather difficult to describe in print the ways of handling rare books; it is simpler to list the ways they should not be handled. The first thing to remember is that books are more fragile than you think they are, not because they are at the moment of touching less sturdy, but because in the expected life span of a book every minute of existence has cut into its future. Many books have survived more than a few centuries of handling, and some of them may be capable of existing almost into infinity (if the present rate of deterioration is not accelerated), but this is not true of all books, or even of most books, and the future is still imponderable.

Therefore, extreme care in handling all rare books is essential. Remembering this point, use common sense and treat all books as though they were as delicate as Venetian lace or a Portland vase. Now, there are certain tricks of handling rare books which a librarian learns very quickly, if he has watched an experienced curator touch his charges. Laugh if you will, but the careful curator keeps his hands clean, even though this is sometimes difficult in a city library. He should expect those who use his books to keep their hands clean also, and especially to remove any traces of grease on the fingers and to keep hands dry.

A book on a shelf is presumably safe from damage as long as it remains on the shelf. Some danger of damage approaches a book when it is removed from its place, and *every removal entails some wear*. This is an inescapable fact, and it should be considered carefully by every curator. For instance, even in libraries where there is the most rigid control of temperature, humidity, and dust, there are, inevitably, particles of dirt in the air which come to rest on the books although they are in locked and presumably airtight cabinets. Even in the best-regulated libraries, some of those particles of dust have fallen between the books on the shelves. As a book is removed from its position on the shelf, the minute, gritty particles are ground into the covers of the book in hand and the covers of the book standing on each side.

Of course, this is a purposeful exaggeration; actually, a book could be removed under the circumstances described a hundred times a year without showing visible scars, but we are dealing with materials which are expected to survive five hundred or a thousand or an unknown number of years, and at some point among the centuries the repeated minute abrasions will destroy the covers. We are all familiar with early sixteenth-century bindings which have been abraded to the point where the lovely blind-stamped patterns are now almost invisible. We have also seen illuminated manuscripts which have been reverently kissed so often that the illumination has all but disappeared.

What to do about it? Nothing now, really, unless protective cases are put on each book, except to remember constantly that the abrasive action is going on each time a book is moved. The rubbing can be minimized if, when a book is removed from its place, the books on either side are moved gently aside. Use two hands when you remove a book from the shelf. With a finger of the right hand placed flat along the top edge, the book can be tipped forward just enough to allow a firm grip on the sides; then, with the left hand, pry the book on either side gently away and draw the book you want out and forward slowly. The rubbing is not wholly eliminated in this way; it is merely minimized.

You will not have time, in a busy rare book collection, to be so careful every time, nor can all rare books be managed in this way, but it is the ideal method to be aimed at and kept in mind; you will be surprised how often it will be found the easiest and best way. Certainly, no book should be removed from a shelf by tugging down on the headcap, or by digging the fingernails into the delicate hinge. There are other problems in removing books from shelves, but they can be solved by the curator if he will use care at all times and remember that rough treatment of any sort damages books. Librarians often find unskilled help useful and desirable for stack work, but they are rarely desirable for rare book sections; in fact, usually they are to be deplored.

To treat books delicately and respectfully when handling them is not difficult to learn; nor is it difficult to treat them in such fashion at all times and to be vigilant where associates and readers are concerned. Be certain to maintain a firm grip on a book while holding it. When you open a book, it is not necessary to bend the covers at the hinges so far back that the fore edges touch; be moderate, neither breaking the back by rough opening nor failing to open the book far enough to read the text easily. A book laid on a table gently will last longer than one slammed down, and, once laid on a table, the book should not be gaily slid over the surface. Handle it gently and respectfully, and it will return your care with longevity.

The "do not's" are many; and, if the curator has the imagination he should have, unnecessary. But let us list a few anyway. Do not dangle a book by a single leaf or a cover—in fact, do not dangle a book. Do not turn a leaf with a damp thumb or finger. In this connection, there are some books so precious and fragile that their leaves should not be turned with the fingers at all. A blunt paper knife, bone folder, or spatula can be used delicately to good advantage in such cases. Do not turn a corner of a leaf down to mark a place, or, for the same purpose, insert a bulky object (comb, pen, scissors, and the like), or place the book, open, face down. Do not place anything on the leaves of the book which will cause a mark or stain. Do not write in a rare book, and do not write on a paper laid on a rare book (cover or text). Never use ink or ball-point pen on or near a rare book. In other words, do not do anything that will in any way damage the book or change it from the condition in which it reached you.

Let there be gentle care and reasonable sense in handling rare books and there will always be rare books. Curators should be ruthless about forbidding careless or uncooperative readers access to the materials in their charge. The curator is responsible for his books; he is charged primarily with their protection from all kinds of damage. Readers should be watched carefully at first, until the curator is certain that the books are being treated with the proper care due them; the reader should then be observed occasionally to be certain that the observed gentle use is habitual and natural. The principle should be laid down early in a curator's career that careless readers will not be tolerated. Often readers will be found who are not accustomed to handling rarities properly; but they can usually be taught easily.

Scholars are often intelligent, even though they are sometimes stubborn.

Most curators have something to say about the books and other materials which are acquired for the collections under their charge, even though their opinions are often heartlessly ignored. A few curators are so unfortunately placed that they are simply housekeepers, being handed acquired goods and told to take care of them, without any share in selection and purchase. It is a pity that so few curators have the privilege of deciding whether or not a certain copy of a desirable book shall be added to a collection, for the curator may be the one individual who knows best what kind of a copy is suitable for a particular collection.

No matter what the source of an object to be added to the rare book collection may be, the first thing the curator must do is examine what he has received through the beneficence of the director of libraries, the whims of the chief of the order department, or the generosity of a benefactor. After all, the material coming in is going to be under the care of the curator and he ought to know what he has. We can assume he knows all there is to know about the contents, or at least as much as he needs to know, and about the bibliographical status, its classification, cataloging, and the like in all the careful details of library processing.

The curator has the serious problem of preserving the book—something ordinary librarians are not trained to know. The curator must have knowledge of what to look for in the physical condition of a book before he plans a campaign for its preservation. There are common points of wear and damage that must be examined before the book is shelved in order to determine what repairs (if any) must be made or planned for in the near future. The experienced curator has established a routine for the examination of a book which may or may not be written out. The first thing he looks at is the first thing he sees—the binding. If the binding is contemporary (original or close to the time of publication), he looks at the covering, no matter what the material used may be. Wear is most frequent at the eight corners, along the top and bottom of the backstrip, and along the hinges. The extent of the damage is noted and assessed. If deterioration is likely to continue rapidly, measures are taken to repair the damage or arrest the process.

On opening the book, he notes the condition of the inner margins and decides whether normal use under good conditions will extend any damage rapidly. He looks at the top, fore, and lower edges of the text to observe the general condition of the leaves (dog-eared? moused? soiled? stained?) and then starts the collation. Whether or not rare books are collated and cataloged in the library's processing department, they should be reexamined by the curator, since catalogers are not always blessed with the special knowledge about rarities that sets the curator apart. He makes certain the maps are the right maps, the plates are the right plates, and the title page belongs to the edition it fronts. During a careful collation defective leaves, soiled leaves, missing leaves, and imperfectly printed or bound leaves will be noted and the necessity for repairs, cleaning, or replacement determined.

Deterioration of a book occurs in both binding and paper. Not a cheerful thought, but true. The whole book deteriorates in time, and some books go to pieces faster than others. Both binding and paper used through the first third of the nineteenth century deteriorate much more slowly than binding and paper used after about 1840. We need not go into the factors which caused this unhappy state of the world of the book manufacturer, except to remark that about the time when publishers began to publish greater quantities of books for a growing reading public, they lowered the standards of bookmaking, and perhaps without realizing it they created problems for later generations of bookmen. Unconsciously the theory of obsolescence of durable goods began its pernicious operations. At any rate, later nineteenth-century books require a good deal more careful examination and handling than their forerunners, for large numbers of them can and do go to pieces quite rapidly.

The curator soon leans the difference between good- and bad-quality paper. Paper with small or no rag content, paper made with unstable chemicals, and paper improperly washed—all tend to become brittle rapidly, and today, even under ideal housing, the time is near when something will have to be done. Note, for instance, a pair of books by Arthur Machen printed during World War I which it is dangerous to touch today, for the paper disintegrates in the fingers. The process is slower in most other books, but the moment is coming when more and more books printed on inferior paper are going to disappear. (Perhaps, in a few instances, it will be advisable to use the Barrow process of "floating" the ink off the original paper and transferring it to fine quality paper.) In any case, the curator must prepare for the worst and face the probability that some books will be lost. That is why the initial examination must be careful and complete and why decisions about the future care of a book must be made at once and carefully pursued.

The repair of books, either the paper or the binding, is almost always possible, as long as substantial portions of the original components are present. The good sense of the curator must determine how extensive the repairs can be and by whom they are to be effected. Some librarians can achieve in time a degree of manual dexterity which will permit them to make minor repairs to bindings and paper; others never reach a state of grace which satisfies them. For the former, it is possible to handle most simple problems, such as worn corners, torn hinges, damaged leaves, and the like. Lydenberg and Archer may be followed in these matters; their book was recently revised by John Alden. It is questionable, however, if the busy curator can afford to give many hours to such time-consuming work. The cost of physical care becomes insupportable when the curator devotes a disproportionate number of hours to such manual tasks.

The employment of a professional binder seems advisable in most

cases, even for minor repairs. Binders accustomed to handling rare
and fragile materials are few and the prices they charge for their work
are high, yet considering time, the cost of time, and the quality of
workmanship, the professional binder is more economical than attempts by the curator to do his own binding and repair. The increasing
number of rare book collections in this country will probably make the
repairing and binding of rare books a profitable business and may encourage young people to become skilled in the craft of binding. Again,
common sense and good judgment must determine what the curator will
do.

Rebinding is an entirely different matter. Such work should not be
attempted by the curator, as this is entirely a matter for the enlight-
ened professional. The work should always be put into the hands of the
best available expert. If the best available is unsatisfactory, the curator would be well-advised to leave the work undone. Rebinding is necessary when a volume is unusable or endangered by use, and it is undertaken only when repair of the original is inadvisable. In the many
ages of the book—manuscript or printed—there have been current
styles of binding, often several styles simultaneously. To preserve or
recapture the style of the contemporary binding ought to be the aim of
the binder. Of course, this is not always possible; the stamped pigskin
binding of the sixteenth century, for instance, or the elaborately tooled
morocco of the seventeenth-century French binder would usually be too
costly to reproduce. If so, the quality of simplicity is desirable, with
the use of appropriate materials wherever possible. For example,
even a plain board binding with backstrip and corners, or backstrip
alone of plain calf on a seventeenth-century book, is preferable to library buckram. On the other hand, simple cloth seems far more appropriate on a nineteenth- or twentieth-century book than a fancy
leather binding.

The sophistication of extremely rare books need not be treated
here, since most curators of collections containing such materials
have already attained a degree of competence which would render this
information useless. It should be apparent that almost anything can be
done to restore a battered copy of a very great rarity from simple repairs to dry cleaning or washing each leaf, replacing margins, and re-
producing in facsimile missing passages, leaves, or sections. The cost
of elaborate repairs, however, added to the original cost of the book
can often mount to more than the purchase price of a fine copy, should
one happen to be available.

We may assume that books acquired by the library and turned over
to a curator already show some wear. The curator's problem is to
prevent continued wear as much as possible. Unless the book is rendered useless by sealing it into an airtight container and never touching it again, further deterioration is inevitable.

Light, heat, and humidity are important factors in the control of the
rate of deterioration. For a longer life, rare books probably should
receive as little light as possible. Strong, natural light, given

continuously, damages books—both binding and paper. Sunlight, for instance, fades and dries both leather and cloth, and if you have worked among books long, the evidence of that statement surrounds you almost every day. Since the chief object of the curator is to conserve the books in his charge as near to the original condition as possible, it is necessary to prevent direct light from falling on them, since books tend to live better in subdued light or no light at all.

Temperature is important to books, too. Unfortunately, they prefer temperatures which most human beings do not so there is a need for compromise, especially if the curator is subject to ailments due to low temperatures. Sixty-five degrees Fahrenheit seems to be the most satisfactory temperature for books of all ages and kinds, but that is a little chilly for human beings, and in deference to the latter, books are normally stored at a slightly higher temperature, between 68° and 75°.

If the relative humidity is maintained at between 45 and 50, books are not likely to suffer. Under such conditions books will neither mold readily nor dry out excessively. Too much aridity or too much moisture can cause serious damage to books, since their effects cannot be eradicated satisfactorily once they have become apparent.

Ideal conditions, of course, are those in which light, temperature, humidity, and dust are under complete control, and the curator is dominated only by the books. Light is fairly easy to control, since most libraries are poorly lit to begin with and interior stacks are notoriously dim and secret places. Temperature and humidity are more difficult to control, and usually a separate system would be necessary for a rare book collection if ideal conditions are to be achieved. There is this consolation, though; most books are hardy objects and have managed to survive under various kinds of abuse. Not all books have stood mistreatment well, but a large number of them have been handed down to us. If ideal conditions are beyond the reach of the curator, he may find it necessary to put up with what he has and hope that the library will eventually get a new building in which proper housing and the necessary equipment will be installed. The remodeling of a single section of an old building is a costly business, and it is usually one which most library technicians are neither willing to try nor able to afford.[1]

Far more serious than the dangers from humidity, temperature, and light are the dangers which come from impurities in the air, and unless the rare book section has been sealed off from the rest of the library, there is not a great deal the curator can do. It is wise to houseclean often and hope for improved equipment. The dangers of polluted air are apparent most frequently on leather-bound books. The leather dries out, becomes powdery, cracks easily, and finally disintegrates. In some cases (particularly in various kinds of nineteenth- and twentieth-century leathers), excessive amounts of acid were used in the rapid processing of the skins and then were not washed out properly.

---

[1] It might be interesting to get a report on the cost and problems encountered when the Newberry Library was renovated during 1961-62.

More commonly, acidic gases in the atmosphere are absorbed by the leather. Most of the gases contain sulfur compounds which are readily taken in and gradually form sulfuric acid. In turn, the sulfuric acid decomposes the leather. Such a deterioration is most frequently found in cities where large quantities of coal, gas, and various other materials containing sulfuric compounds are regularly burned.

The deleterious effects of sulfuric acid can be minimized somewhat by paying special attention to individual bindings. An application of potassium lactate (7 percent solution) to a leather surface will neutralize the sulfuric acid. This should be followed by one of the recommended leather dressings which, while it will not protect the leather from acid decay, will delay the decay and help to restore to the leather some of the oils which have been lost through slow and long-time drying. In recent years scientists and librarians have been attempting to devise a dressing for leather which will incorporate a buffering agent so that the two operations will be effected simultaneously. Progress has been made, and there is reason to hope that the chemists now at work on the problem will succeed in perfecting a product.

The varieties of dressings are many, and each has its adherents. It is not necessary to discuss them here as they are described (with formulae) by Lydenberg and Archer and by Plenderleith, both of which are listed in the Selected Bibliography at the end of this book. It should be noted, perhaps, that a simple preparation of neat's-foot oil and anhydrous lanolin applied approximately every three years over a period of thirty years has left the books so treated in a highly satisfactory condition. The preparation has a fairly unpleasant odor when fresh, but a few drops of cedarwood oil will make it more agreeable to smell and add a scent that is not unpleasant to most people.

There is very little one can do with safety and satisfaction to improve the appearance of other kinds of binding materials, except to keep them clean and as free as possible from dust and dirt. The judicious use of soft erasers will do wonders to many paper-covered or board-bound volumes, but beyond this kind of "dry cleaning" nothing should be done. The use of water on clothbound books, particularly those with sized cloth, is unwise. Some librarians are now recommending the use of acrylic lacquers for the protection of paper, cloth, and leather bindings. It is doubtful that enough time has passed since this process was introduced to be certain that the claims made for lacquers are justified. Lacquered surfaces are certainly easier to clean than untreated surfaces, and dirt and stains do not penetrate them easily. Acrylic lacquers, usually applied in spray form, have been tried successfully to shed dirt from fabrics (chair seats, rugs, and the like) and, by artists, as fixatives for chalk, charcoal, pencil, and pastel drawings. Whether or not they will eventually discolor the surfaces they now protect has not been determined.

Cleanliness, as I have stressed, is the chief guard against the rapid deterioration of rare books. If you can keep the air clean, well and good; if not, careful and frequent cleaning is essential. Where dust is a serious problem (and this is nearly everywhere), books should be removed from the shelves annually and cleaned individually, preferably with a small, hand vacuum cleaner with very long, soft bristles on the nozzle. Dislodge the dust gently with the bristles and let the vacuum carry it away. Never clap books together with a sharp bang to dislodge the dust. Just as important, never press the dirt into the surface or between the leaves by dusting with a rough cloth or stiff brush. Some librarians still use feather dusters; it is a little difficult to damage a book with a feather duster, but all that is accomplished is a redistribution of the dust which has been in the collection for years. Shelves under the books and the interior walls of the shelves should be cleaned at the same time, preferably (if the surface finish will stand it) with a slightly dampened cloth. The shelves and walls should be dry before the books are returned to their places.

Rare book collections are generally highlighted by a few (or many) spectacular rarities which require special attention, and these are usually separately housed in a properly constructed vault or locked room. Sometimes a collection may contain materials so fragile that unusual precautions must be taken to ensure their continued existence. Most books and pamphlets with these characteristics may be protected adequately and allowed to take their places on the shelves if they are enclosed individually within protective cases. There are many varieties of cases, from simple board folders to elaborate leather-covered solander cases. Plain board or paper folders to protect the sides and backstrips are never really satisfactory, and solander cases are usually too elaborate or expensive to be feasible. Between these extremes, however, there are two varieties of protective cases which will serve adequately in nearly every instance where special protection is required.

One of these is the hinged box, formed in the shape of a book and covered in a suitable book material (boards, cloth, with or without leather backstrip). Slightly less expensive is a simple open-end case with inner cloth folder. For each kind the fit of the book within the case should be snug but not tight. To handle some problems, such as a 45-pound quarto manuscript volume which is going to be used quite often, special cases can be designed and executed by an experienced binder.

The curator who is sympathetic toward rare books and who uses common sense is the surest protection against continued rapid deterioration of the materials under his charge. We may envisage the ideal setting for a rare book collection and aim for it, but the ideal is, for most of us, impossible of attainment. We must therefore compromise—always, of course, in favor of the books.

The handling of manuscripts is not essentially different from the handling of rare books, except that even greater precautions must be taken against accidental destruction. Manuscripts are, for the most part, unique, and if they are destroyed they cannot be replaced, as a rare book often can be. Additional precautions must be taken, particularly with readers who, accustomed to tougher books, treat unique treasures with a certain casualness. Most of the strictures on handling books described earlier in this chapter are equally applicable to manuscripts.

When manuscripts reach the curator, they should be examined carefully for defects. Most commonly, the earliest signs of wear appear at the folds of the manuscript; in lesser degree, wear is apparent at the outer edges. Seriously frayed outer edges should be repaired if further damage is likely to occur through use. An original letter is usually written on paper which has been folded at least once. Continued opening and folding of paper weakens the fibers—minutely each time, it is true, but weakens them nevertheless—and it is wise to guard against further opening and refolding by keeping the letter as flat as is practicable. A four-page quarto letter, i.e., a folio sheet folded once to make four pages, is the commonest kind of letter with which curators must deal. The single fold will stand a good deal of wear and may be left until it begins to break, at which time it may be hinged or supported by a narrow strip of tough paper. Additional folds, such as those made by folding the letter for insertion in an envelope, should be smoothed out. Stubborn folds may be minimized by the judicious use of a gently warmed electric iron.

The frayed edges of manuscript leaves are more difficult to repair and probably should be left to the more experienced hands of a professional binder. This is also true of leaves broken at the folds. But before the manuscript is sent to the binder, there are some things the curator and his assistants can do. For instance, the manuscripts are often dirty when they arrive in the library, particularly when they come straight from an old garret. The curator can clean them by shaking or blowing on them to remove the loose dust and by carefully erasing the dirt which may be more difficult to remove. Stains which have penetrated below the surface of the paper should be treated by a professional binder. In some cases, manuscripts sent to the library are buggy, wormy, mildewed, or too brittle to handle; then special techniques must be called into play, such as fumigating and cleaning, which are beyond the abilities of most curators and should be left to experts. Any curator will be grateful to receive manuscripts (or books, for that matter) which have not been repaired with plastic tape.

There are several ways to protect fragile manuscripts which have been improperly treated by their former owners and are therefore in danger of total destruction. The most elaborate method (suitable only for really spectacular pieces) is to encase the manuscript in a glass receptacle or case in which the ordinary air has been replaced with an inert gas. This is an expensive process and is reserved for such uniquities as the Declaration of Independence and similar documents. More practical is the preservation of single leaves of manuscripts by pressing them tightly between sheets of flexible glass or plastic welded or riveted together. Less expensive and suitable for all except show pieces are the processes of silking, laminating, and mounting. The silking of manuscripts is relatively safe, if good materials are used. An extremely thin layer of fine, transparent silk gauze is pasted to each side of a manuscript and dried under pressure. It is unwise to fold a silked manuscript; the silk fibers, stiffened with paste, break easily. The silking will last for many years, although in time the paste will dry out completely and the silk will come loose.

In the best process of lamination, a thin layer of transparent plastic film plus a tissue are welded to each side of the manuscript by applying heat and pressure. The process has been in use for more than twenty-five years and, when properly done, appears to give permanent protection to the manuscripts. If the paper shows an undesirable acid content, it should receive an alkaline treatment before lamination. The National Archives, so far as I can determine, still approves of the process and uses it. Incidentally, the plastic can be removed. Mounting a manuscript on fine quality paper, when writing appears on only one side of the paper, is a simple and effective method of strengthening the original paper. Cellulose acetate envelopes, sealed on three sides, provide adequate protective coverings for frequently used manuscripts. Satisfactory methods of handling manuscripts in bulk are described in Howard H. Peckham's excellent article in the *American Archivist*.[2]

Collections of manuscripts, when small and composed of heterogeneous materials, are most easily stored either in filing cabinets or in boxes constructed for the purpose. In either case, the individual manuscripts may be hinged along the inner edge to sheets of fairly stiff paper of uniform size. The separate pieces are then easily manageable in bulk. With a tough, thin paper or a lightweight cotton cloth as a hinge, the original manuscript may be attached to a sheet of fine paper measuring about 15 inches by 12 inches. Each manuscript should then be inserted in a slightly larger folder (also of good, acid-free paper) and filed in the appropriate container. It is satisfactory to use file boxes, which make good containers, or print boxes about 2 inches thick; both varieties are available commercially and are easily labeled. The print boxes are ordinarily laid flat in stacks of two or three to a pile. Transfer file boxes may be stored in the same way or, if they are comfortably filled, may be placed upright just as books are shelved.

The manuscript collection should be protected in some kind of closed case to prevent soiling and contact with strong light. Most writing inks fade when exposed to natural light over a long period. It is therefore inadvisable to exhibit manuscripts, regardless of age, longer than about thirty days and then, preferably, only in artificial light which is, of course, somewhat safer. Tests have indicated that manuscripts may be protected from natural or artificial light by filter glass or filter plastics.

Collections of related manuscripts—the surviving papers of an individual, for instance—to which additions are not expected may be bound

[2] Howard H. Peckham, "Arranging and Cataloguing Manuscripts in the William L. Clements Library," *American Archivist*, 1:215-29 (Oct. 1938).

in volumes of suitable size. The individual manuscripts should be hinged to large sheets of acid-free paper, arranged in chronological or alphabetical order, and then bound. Usually, a volume of sixty to eighty manuscripts tipped to sheets of large folio size will remain manageable. Under no circumstances should collections of manuscripts be bound without protective mounting sheets (acid-free) separating the individual manuscripts. Manuscripts should not be folded in a bound volume, i.e., if a single manuscript is too long for the size of the volume used, the lower edge should not be folded up. Either use a larger size of volume or separate the single piece from the collection before binding.

As with books, the protection of manuscripts depends on the good sense of the curator and on careful attention to housekeeping. The curator who proceeds carefully and cautiously and with the advice and counsel of skilled technicians will eventually hand over to his successor a collection which may last for centuries. Only continued judicious care will ensure the safety of rare materials for the use of future generations of bookmen, scholars, and librarians.[3]

---

[3] This chapter has been designed to state certain principles of the conservation of rare materials. It is not designed as a text or set of instructions on technical problems. It was written on the assumption that curators would investigate techniques carefully before applying them to the books and manuscripts under their control.

Chapter VIII

Physical Housing and Equipment

NEAL R. HARLOW

As it may now seem less marvelous that Columbus discovered America than incredible that he could have missed it, so the mysteries which this chapter reveals may appear less striking to the diligent reader than that much of it is so familiar. The New World, however, was once a barrier on the route to Asia, and we heedfully set in the path of the inquirer whatever seems most useful.

The world of the fifteenth century was round but much farther around than anyone supposed, and the modern librarian's sphere is vaster in scope than many bookmen know. One of the less-frequented corners of librarianship is considered in some detail below. No attempt is made to offer specific answers to a mass of practical questions, but approaches will surely be opened to many local problems.

Special library facilities should be planned to satisfy the following general principles: They should be specifically designed for the use they are intended to serve. They should allow for growth and expansion. They should support efficient and economical administration. They should provide for the proper storage and handling of materials, for essential supervision, and for a convenient relationship between the user and the collection. They should be as attractive as possible and be constructed for a price which is within the funds available. Much of library economy will be embraced in efforts to achieve these objectives.

The responsibility of a special department is to handle rare, unusual, fragile, and special materials. They must be acquired, received, processed, and stored; protected from theft, damage, and deterioration; and made available for use when required. Preservation and use for scholarly purposes is the objective of the whole operation—often within a wider institutional pattern—and a variety of relationships within and outside the special department must be carefully considered.

LOCATION

In establishing a rare book room or department of special collections, physical location requires early and primary attention. If the specialized department will not be used by large groups or by the public generally, it should be outside the circle of heavy traffic, and attempts should not be made to attract numbers of people to it (for example, by staging popular exhibitions inside the area). Nevertheless, the services of general reference, bibliography, loan, serials, receiving and processing, binding, and photography will be constantly required to supplement the department's resources, and one should not be too far removed from the others. The existence of convenient stairways and elevators, of telephones and intercommunication systems, of pneumatic tubes, book conveyers, or other such facilities will help to bring the department within the larger orbit. As a unit of a larger research organization, the department should be as well coordinated with the other divisions as the local compromise between demands and services permits.

Some of the operations associated with the conservation and use of unusual research materials necessitate a greater self-sufficiency than is required by most library departments. Physical security is the primary responsibility, modified only by the necessity to make the materials available to competent users in the most convenient manner consistent with continuing use. Security (to have more attention later) is of several kinds, involving protection not only from theft but from fire, moisture, desiccation, chemical action, dust, abrasion, rough handling, light, insects, bacteria, fungus, and any other deleterious influence. Add to these particular responsibilities a strong emphasis upon conditions favorable to use (ample light and air, special equipment, supervised study space, and a staff with technical and subject competence), and requirements exist which differ in kind and degree from those which are characteristic of other parts of the organization.

EQUIPMENT AND FACILITIES

Incoming materials may be received and processed by the specialized staff as well as by the general departments. Manuscripts are most likely to be handled in this way, and archives, pamphlets, perhaps maps, and rare books as well, if standards of security or of bibliographic description are not met elsewhere. In large departments of this kind, binding and repair, and sometimes photography, may be segregated, since work on rare, fragile, or other unusual material may not be done properly under normal shop conditions. Indeed there are numerous examples of a complete separation of rare book libraries and their processes from other local facilities for reasons not necessarily related to use and conservation.

Separate catalogs, bibliographies, finding lists, calendars, guides, reference works, and other keys to special resources may also be provided. Full advantage should be taken of research materials available in an adjacent general library, but dependence should not penalize work in fields of special concentration whenever duplication of material is practicable. Carrels, typing rooms, microreaders and printers, ultraviolet lamps, even collating machines, are characteristic furnishings of such laboratory-libraries.

In a department of this kind the claims of the user for attention come second to those of the research materials, but since the reader and his many successors provide the motive for collecting and preservation, the library must conscientiously cater to his interests. Study space must be adequate in size, comfortable, well lighted and ventilated, and quiet and convenient to the materials required. If individual work desks are provided (no smaller than 2-1/2 feet x 4 feet), some larger tables should be available for special needs. Chairs should support the user in a working, not a lounging, position and be related to table height. Closed study carrels are desirable for continuing projects, though their use will need to be restricted to reputable scholars. Well-distributed general lighting (50-80 foot-candles at present standards, measurements to be taken a month after installation) in a room which is itself light in color is desirable for the close scrutiny of printed and manuscript sources. Panels of light which allow plenty of illumination to spill over onto the surrounding ceiling (to avoid contrast) give good diffusion if they are not separated by a wider space than two adjacent fixtures can illuminate.

Fluorescent tubes, screened by plastic or some type of "egg crate" louver, have virtually replaced incandescent globes. They no longer need to flicker, start slowly, or be noisy; they are long lived and are available in warm or cool colors. Heating and ventilating louvers are often placed in the areas between light panels; and all of the space not covered by these units, as well as selected areas of the walls, should be acoustically treated. A great variety of surface material is available to absorb sound, other than the overly familiar acoustic tile made of perforated squares, some of the most effective of which takes advantage of dead air space. Ceiling height has a modifying effect upon lighting, ventilation, and acoustical needs.

The reader should be placed in a convenient relationship to the catalogs, reference works, and public desk. If the department has been well situated in respect to general library facilities, this, too, will greatly facilitate his work.

Staff as well as functions and furnishings should contribute to the distinct and self-sufficient character of the department. Above all the staff members should be bookish, scholarly, and sound reference librarians, respecting the book as an object as well as a record, capable in research, and interested in helping others to exploit library materials. The department also has a responsibility for public relations—to attract additions to the library and to make its resources known—and the staff will express these interests through the exercise of diverse talents. The resourcefulness of the staff in making known and exploiting outside facilities for the benefit of users is an important asset, and functioning relationships between the department and appropriate libraries, archives, and private collections should be purposefully worked out. The department head should occupy a position of respect which is second to none in the literary and scholarly community.

BURGLARY AND FIRE PREVENTION

The physical organization and arrangement of the department must clearly recognize and support the special administrative responsibilities. Both security and economy require the control of incoming and outgoing traffic, the use of material within the area, and access to the closed stack and to the general book collection, if an entrance to the latter is located in the department. Supervision has psychological as well as direct physical aspects, and it need not always be obvious when the user is under observation. Room exits should be well separated from other facilities so that persons may not mask their intentions when upon the point of departure. A second exit to the reading room, if required by law, should be provided with an emergency exit lock which sounds an alarm when opened irregularly.

Outside the hours of public service, dependence must be put upon burglar- and fire-alarm systems, police protection, and the careful control of keys. Automatic warning systems (based upon breaking an electrical circuit), supplemented by manual switches at the public desk to set off an alarm, are standard equipment. It should be noted that routine rounds made by watchmen are easily avoided by an observant thief. Keys for the department should be on a separate master or above the level of master keys available to other departments, and most keys should remain in the library when it is closed. A minimum of maintenance personnel should have free access. A secondary steel vault door, with combination lock, can be installed to protect the bookstack when the department is closed. Quarters should preferably not be on the ground floor or basement level where they may incite intrusion, and even somewhat higher levels should be screened to thwart breaking-in and dropping material from open windows.

Fire protection should not take the form of automatic sprinkling equipment, since damage is more likely from water than from fire. Manual or heat-operated fire-alarm systems are essential, although the best protection is fireproof construction. The dry type of portable fire extinguisher (sodium bicarbonate) is less damaging, reasonably effective, and most appropriate for books and paper, and fog more satisfactory than spray nozzles for standpipes which may be required by law in corridors and reading rooms. Standard steel bookstack construction has a low fire-resistance rating because of its exposed steel columns, and the use, therefore, of special insulation in walls or doors adds little to underwriter's requirements. Under most circumstances money spent upon special vaults might be better invested in improving general fireproofing. Nitrate film, inflammable solvents, waxes and cleaners, waste paper, and other fire hazards should not be allowed to stand in the department. Close cooperation with local authorities in regard to fire protection and extinction should be maintained.

PRESERVATION

An important aid to preservation is air conditioning, and for the storage area it is of major concern. By controlling air flow and distribution, temperature, humidity, dust, gases (particularly sulphur dioxide), and bacteria, most of the damage arising from factors other than use can be kept in check (insects and rodents require other kinds of attention). Full air conditioning is a complex and expensive process, and no attempt will be made to discuss it fully here. Compact units are being manufactured for use in given areas, including electrostatic dust control (the precipitron is expensive to install but is the most effective of the various filtering methods). Since smoke requires a large amount of circulated air to dissipate, smoking necessitates the use of a more expensive system of greater capacity than would otherwise be needed; for this and other reasons smoking should not be permitted in the rare book department.

A variety of special equipment is available for handling or preserving printed and manuscript materials and should be familiar to specialized staff. Boxes and folders for filing manuscripts, pamphlets, broadsides, and maps should be made of a chemically inert substance. Such materials are ideally stored in a horizontal position (storage boxes with hinged covers and drop-down fronts for ease of access are available), but they may be shelved vertically if contents are well supported. Archival papers are often stored in vertical boxes which depend simply upon fullness to prevent curling of material. Such equipment should be as lightproof and dustproof as possible. Rare maps should be stored flat.

The composition and use of solutions for the preservation of leather bindings were treated in the previous chapter; deterioration can only be retarded, not actually repaired, and treatment should be carried out early and regularly. Lamination is a highly specialized process and should not be applied to important material without expert guidance. Cleaners, treated dustcloths, waxes, and other preparations should not be used until after proper testing and investigation.

ADMINISTRATION

The physical arrangements within the department will govern the ease and cost of administration. The control of access and use is discussed in the next chapter; supervision, to be feasible with a minimum staff under average conditions, should be possible from a single point. The reference function must also center there, with ready access to the public catalog, reference books, work space, bookstack, and reading room, and to the elevators, stairways, and communication systems. Such fundamental physical objects as electric switches, wash basin, work tables, clock, and toilet should be in convenient positions in order to minimize periods of absence from the desk. Ample space for every phase of the operation should be provided, with opportunity to expand all of them. Book storage should be expendable into existing or proposed stack space, and reading room areas into adjacent seminar rooms, carrel space, or future additions. Physical facilities should be planned with the use of human beings in mind or they will be only partially effective, and funds and energy wasted upon administration cannot be spent upon other resources. A library, like an individual, may develop a distinct, even memorable, personality, compounded of its bibliographical, physical, administrative, and human qualities.

This chapter, like a general chart of the world, indicates only the chief surface features, showing where the main routes and hazards lie, and a traveler wishing to browse around in a chosen local area should look for details upon a sheet of much larger scale. Meanwhile, if he has been saved from a few sunken rocks and weird monsters, he may, like Columbus, have bumped into a great many more important facts of life on the way.

Chapter IX

Access, Service, and Publications

HANNAH D. FRENCH

For reasons already presented in previous chapters, materials in special collections should not be looked upon as expendable. Security must be given a first consideration in any library that maintains a department of rare books. Consequently every possible means for their security must be used before reference service or any type of circulation is considered. Protection from physical damage is of paramount concern; methods of protection to prevent theft and careless use are equally important in this matter of preserving rare materials.

SECURITY

Within the last few decades entirely new concepts of the importance of preserving books and documents from physical damage have developed. Control of their environment is now considered basic. The fireproof building which was once looked upon as the ultimate protection is now only the first step. To combat the natural forces of decay, techniques of air conditioning have been improved during the past twenty-five years, and now the ideal systems provide excellent control of temperature and of humidity, and air-filtering units supply a modern building with air that is virtually free of noxious gases and corrosive elements.

In the years since World War II, bombproof vaults have been installed in a few of the greatest rare book libraries. For example, in 1951, the Henry E. Huntington Library in California completed its bombproof area, encased in steel and concrete, 12 feet below ground. In addition to Harvard's Houghton Library, the Lilly Library at Indiana University (one of the most recent important separate buildings for rare books) has installed proven scientific equipment providing air conditioning, air filtering, and so-called bombproof vaults. At the same time many of the older institutions have equipped their buildings with air conditioning and air filtering, which engineers consider essential for the preservation of rare, valuable, and other special materials. One recent example of a new installation in an old building is that of the library of the Union Theological Seminary in the heart of New York City.

Protection of the contents of rare book collections was considered as a problem long before the advent of the present scientific controls of their environment. Over the years much study and thought have gone into the preservation of leather bindings and of paper. The study of deterioration of leather began early in the century, and various formulae for the treatment of leather bindings have been published. Though very few libraries attain the ideal of oiling their leather bindings every six months, it is not from lack of knowledge that they fail to do so. This type of care has been publicized over a number of years. The most useful book on the subject, Lydenberg and Archer's *Care and Repair of Books*, has appeared in four editions. It was first published by Bowker in 1931 and was revised by John Alden for the fourth edition (1960).

The proper treatment of fragile paper documents has been studied more recently, but it is more difficult to find material about lamination, about acid-free papers to be used to make folders for valuable letters and documents, and about the possible harmful effects of cellophane wrappers and envelopes. These studies come within the province of the National Archives in conjunction with the National Bureau of Standards, and we are indebted to those agencies for their research on preservation and rehabilitation. This is a continuing study and more important than the study of bindings in that the very life of much rare material depends upon the preservation of paper, whereas bindings can be replaced and often are. If it is not deemed practical or advisable to replace original bindings which have been severely damaged, the book and what remains of its binding can be protected indefinitely by placing it in a box case made to order by the binder. Just as it was the fashion to rebind first editions in elegant, decorated leather bindings in the nineteenth century, it is a present-day tendency bordering on a fetish to preserve whatever remains of the original binding though it be only a few shreds.

As long ago as 1937, *Books & Documents,* by Julius Grant, was published in England and the United States. The subtitle, "Dating, Permanence, and Preservation," indicated the scope of the book. This work gives a careful, full presentation of what was known on the subject at that time and can be studied to advantage in conjunction with two recent books, H. J. Plenderleith's *The Conservation of Antiquities and Works of Art: Treatment, Repair, and Restoration,* published by Oxford in 1956, and W. H. Langwell's *The Conservation of Books and Documents,* published by Pitman in 1957. These and other recommended titles are listed in the Selected Bibliography at the end of this book.

Protection against theft has been a consideration of first importance since ancient times. As the problem of theft is always a serious matter, certain means of protection must be devised. In most libraries the rare book area is often set apart and provided with appropriate and sufficient locks. Exhibition cases should be kept locked, as should all glass bookcases in the rare book room. The air-conditioned bookstack, which has replaced the old-fashioned vault in many larger libraries, should have a lock or a combination, or both. Although there is a qualified attendant in the rare book room, the entrance and exits may be kept locked. This is not the usual practice, but it is the custom in the reserve room at the New York Public Library and at Houghton, Clark, and other libraries.

Yet, in spite of these many forms of protection, thefts have taken place (but not necessarily at the institutions where the fullest protective measures are employed). For instance, the Whitman manuscript notebook was stolen from the Detroit Public Library a few years ago, when the exhibition case containing it was pried open and the item removed by an unknown "borrower." It may be necessary to employ guards, as museums do, whenever the library exhibition contains material on loan. Few libraries, however, have the need for guards on a permanent basis, and the cost of this kind of protection is prohibitive in all but certain large and particularly valuable collections.

Not all thefts have taken place because no attendant was present. There have been examples of embarrassing thefts made by readers more or less under the eye of the custodian. One thinks back to February, 1940, to the disappearance of the Shakespeare First Folio at Chapin Library, Williams College, filched by a small-time thief who had succeeded in masquerading as a visiting scholar by presenting a forged letter of introduction. At the University of California at Los Angeles, in 1952, a copy of the Bay Psalm Book was actually spirited out of the exhibition gallery at night, but the thief was apprehended as he ran from the building.

Protection from vandals is equally important. Indeed, vandals may do as much permanent damage as thieves. In the cases of thefts mentioned above, the articles were returned safely, or were recovered after a period of time. As there is seldom a ready market for stolen rarities, except in unusual cases, few valuable items return to the dealers for sale to unwary buyers. Vandalism is less easily detected, but oftentimes the results are irreparable. Books have been hopelessly mutilated while being used within the library. The classic example remains to be fully exposed when the studies of the activities of Thomas J. Wise are completed and published. Mr. Wise seems to have been a master of nefarious practices in the book world. Many counterfeit first editions "discovered" by Wise were exposed in Carter and Pollard's *Enquiry into the Nature of Certain Nineteenth-Century Pamphlets,* in 1934, and now we have sufficient evidence to show that these productions may be but part of a much larger life of crime rather than a brief and inexplicable excursion into it. Critical and bibliographical investigations may reveal information about Mr. Wise's activity in removing leaves from copies of certain seventeenth-century plays in the British Museum for the purpose of bettering his own defective copies. A

reader of more innocent appearance than Thomas J. Wise would be
hard to imagine.

For many years it seemed that the New York Public Library prac-
ticed necessary precautions for the surveillance and inspection of
books, but not long ago even this sanctorum was proved vulnerable to
the dismay of many members of the library staff as well as of out-
siders. Readers and librarians, unmindful of such historical events,
may not approve of strict regulations requiring all rare materials to
be used in the reading room before the door is unlocked to let the user
out of the room. Any curator, familiar with numerous cases of recent
years, knows that he must be ever alert to prevent thefts and acts of
vandalism where irreplaceable materials are concerned.

Thieves or vandals who deliberately masquerade as serious readers can scarcely be classified as "careless users." There are readers, however, who may cause much damage to valuable materials
through their own ignorance and lack of careful instruction. To guard
against these, certain precautions are usually effective; they include
specific regulations to which the user of the rare book room must
agree. The rules require the identification of readers: by letter, by
application forms, by conference and registration, or by a combination
of these methods. Such a record serves to identify the person and tells
what materials he wishes to use and for what purposes.

All readers should be supervised by some staff member who will
refer the reader to the rules for the use of materials which are posted
or issued in a printed leaflet; or it may be necessary to explain ver-
bally regulations with regard to certain materials. These may vary in
importance from the simple rule forbidding the use of ink to the requirement of written permission if the reader wishes to publish any
material that is restricted for any reason. The rules should be simple
but carefully presented. The late Randolph Adams, in his classic essay
"Librarians as Enemies of Books," made many challenging observations on the misdemeanors of librarians, labeling as one enemy of
books "the librarian who allows rare books to be used without proper
restrictions."[1]

INSURANCE

Expecting to maintain maximum security without carrying proper
insurance is unthinkable when a library is attempting to preserve materials which would be very difficult, if not impossible, to replace.
The insurance on a large general collection of books is one thing; insurance for rare books and manuscripts quite another. Until a few
years ago the insurance for the latter called for an entirely different
type of policy. That is, special and rare materials were insured under
an all-risk policy, customarily a Fine Arts Policy, which was also used

---

[1] Randolph G. Adams, "Librarians as Enemies of Books," *Library Quarterly*, 7:317
ff. (July 1937).

for paintings, valuable rugs, statuary, and other similar property. The
protection given by such a policy covers not only fire, but also mali-
cious mischief, burglary, windstorm, theft, explosion, earthquake, riot,
and almost every conceivable danger except war risk. It also covers
materials while they are not in the custody of the institution that owns
them, as when lent for exhibition, sent out for repairs, or for any other
purpose. This may be handled on a percentage basis, which is to say
that items valued at no more than 10 percent of the total policy can be
insured at any one time. This places the limit on what can be sent out
on loan or for repairs at a figure which may be sufficient for most institutions.

In 1941 a Valuable Papers Policy was first offered, especially designed for libraries and for collections of rare books and manuscripts.
Like the Fine Arts Policy, it requires a rather complete listing of the
insured articles and their values. It is described in some detail by C.
W. Mixer in his article, "New Insurance for Library Collections."[2]
Mr. Mixer explains fully how this policy can be made to apply to both
collections if desired—both the special collections which are itemized
and the general collections which are not.

Listing each item and giving it a value is a demanding and time-
consuming task. It presupposes capability and enough free time at the
disposal of staff members to assure proper attention to minute details.
Frequently the librarian or the custodian of the collection finds it necessary to engage the services of a reputable dealer to get appraisals.
Sometimes a compromise is effected by setting an arbitrary minimum
value at $500 or more. In any case, the list should be checked over in
detail with the reputable insurance broker who will handle the insurance. Furthermore, it may be wise to make reappraisals at periodic
intervals whenever auction records or sales catalogs indicate changes
in values, or when the collections increase in size.

As matters of security are important factors to prospective donors,
they affect the responsibilities of the administrative officers at any institution where gifts of rare and valuable materials are acquired. Such
responsibilities involve the proper housing of materials to ensure maximum protection from physical damage and protection against theft,
and a special insurance commensurate with the value of the collections
in the event of catastrophe. These responsibilities are shared by the
members of the staff who are charged with the duties of caring for and
supervising the use of the library's property. Everyone so employed
must exercise the necessary precautions to prevent theft, vandalism,
and careless use as well as the natural results of the ravages of time.

REFERENCE SERVICE

In rare book collections today perhaps the use of the materials is
the greatest challenge. Acquisition and preservation of materials must

---

[2] C. W. Mixer, "New Insurance for Library Collections," *Library Journal*, 79:1539-
43 (Sept. 15, 1954).

come first; but reference service must follow closely, for it is the signpost to use, actual and potential. The personal knowledge, initiative, and imagination of the rare book librarian and staff are important in making available the fullest use of the materials under their care. This knowledge they continually increase by study and by interchange of information with the scholars, collectors, and rare book dealers with whom they are familiar. They make use of all existing printed aids such as bibliographies, indexes, and catalogs with many entries and indexes. The catalogs of booksellers and auction houses are their daily or, more probably, bedtime reading.

Fortified by all these resources librarians serve as a clearinghouse for information, or as "integrators of knowledge" as Mark Van Doren expressed it in an unpublished lecture. They answer bibliographical inquiries, often intricate ones, by letter; they provide photostats or microfilm for the scholar who is unable to come in person; they show off the "crown jewels" to casual visitors, exhibiting the collection according to the varied tastes of the visitors; and they prepare exhibitions on many subjects, often pointing out potential use of their collections by this means. They may even provide hand lists or catalogs of their most important exhibitions.

The idea of service seizes the imagination as the older, purely custodial concept never could. Paul Angle once wrote: "...reference work in the rare book room is reference work of the most exacting kind. Those who do it, and do it well, must be steeped in the knowledge of books outside and in and skilled in making them give up their informational yield under handicaps unthought of in the general reference room...In a word, they will themselves be rare...they will also be of that select company who find contentment, even happiness, in their daily work."[3] The rare book librarian does find particular happiness in the reference service that he performs. Lawrence Wroth has written of the added privilege in giving "a peculiar service" to all bookmen which is the increased responsibility in the special library, and closes his remarks with the reminder that "with institutions as with men life without service is life without meaning."[4]

The great curators have always put their extensive personal knowledge and their inspired memories at the service of their readers. To a student who some twenty years ago was working in the Morgan Library when Miss Belle da Costa Greene presided there the experience will be forever remembered.

Today's curator has access to a vast number of practical aids, ordinary and extraordinary. These include bibliographies, catalogs, indexes, finding lists, and other reference tools in print and near print. If he does not have a thorough knowledge of collections elsewhere as

---

[3] Paul Angle, "Reference Work in the Rare Book Room," in Pierce Butler, ed., *The Reference Function of the Library* (Chicago: Univ. of Chicago Pr., 1943), p.298.

[4] Lawrence C. Wroth, "A Negation and Some Affirmations," in Howard H. Peckham, ed., *Library Trends*, 5:425 (April 1957).

well as in his own library, he at least knows how they may be found
through bibliographies and union catalogs and can thus be of invaluable
assistance to scholars and to students pursuing specific subjects. His
services are available, also, to book collectors, bibliographers, or
even to casual visitors who become ecstatic over a fore-edge painting
—in short, to all who come to study or to marvel.

The reference tools established and maintained by the curator and
his staff will be extremely useful. These will include sheet catalogs
for the most valuable and interesting items for which there is too much
detailed information to go on catalog cards. Catalog cards will either
give detailed information or refer to the sheet catalogs. There may be
special card files for autographs, binders, bookplates, donors, printers,
illustrators, private presses, and the like. The early books—fifteenth
and sixteenth century, at least—will be covered by chronological files
and files for the names of printers and the places they worked.

General reference and bibliographical material is often duplicated
in the rare book reading room, and this is important to the scholar who
has come for a short visit and must make every minute count. Auction
catalogs, the catalogs of rare book dealers, and auction records are
usually shelved there, also, or close at hand, as the information they
contain is frequently needed.

The visiting scholar may not require photostats or microfilm. He
may prefer to bring his own photographic equipment with him and make
his own reproductions. For the many scholars and students who are
unable to make a journey, however, photostats and microfilm are of
primary importance. A photographic department for the making of
microfilms and photostats in the building, or nearby, is more of a necessity today than a convenience, unless one can get friendly and prompt
service at a neighboring institution (as Wellesley does at Widener Library, a dozen miles away). Fortunately, the Xerox equipment on the
campus and the Contoura machine in the library can take care of much
of the increasing demand for photocopies.

EXHIBITIONS

Various exhibitions of rare materials also serve an important reference function. This is particularly true in the college and university
library, where exhibitions are frequently arranged at the request of a
professor, or in cooperation with an instructor, to serve the curriculum. At Williams College such an exhibition was valued so highly as a
teaching instrument by one professor that he included a question based
upon it in the course examination from year to year. Equally interesting and valuable are the exhibitions which help to cut across depart-
mentalized knowledge and to introduce students and faculty to subjects
not included in the curriculum.

A successful exhibition at Wellesley, "Italian Influence on English
Poetry of the Renaissance," interweaving material from the Plimpton
Collection of Italian Literature and the English Poetry Collection,

brought together significant material from two important collections
for the Renaissance Society at its annual meeting on the campus.
Wellesley presents periodically exhibitions on "The Art of the Book,"
"Book Collecting," "The Fifty Books of the Year," "Catalogues of
Great Private Book Collections," and other phases of the book arts, as
its own special contribution, so that no student need leave college unaware of the history of the book, the aesthetic value of well-printed
books, the joy of collecting and building a personal library, and the
great service performed by serious collectors for posterity—in short,
unacquainted with book madness.

Exhibitions—representing, as they do, selections of materials on a
given subject significantly displayed with descriptive notes—are a distinct reference service to the community which is able to view them at
first hand. Printed catalogs, if they can be provided, exploit the reference value of an exhibition by providing a permanent record for the
viewer and making the same material available to any persons who
have been unable to visit the library.

There are two distinct types of exhibitions. One includes items
collected from various sources, and the other assembles materials
from a single permanent collection. In this age of mobility exhibitions
may be assembled from materials all over the world. A record of rarities brought together from various collections for one brief period of
time may be of priceless reference value for the scholar and for the
collector. With the Blake anniversary of 1957 and its spate of exhibition catalogs one thinks back to the Blake exhibition of 1939, held in
Philadelphia, as an early and ambitious attempt at this kind of exhibition. No Blake collection of importance should be without the catalog
of that exhibition, or without the many catalogs accompanying exhibitions during the bicentennial exhibitions of 1957.

To honor the memory of Dr. Johnson on the 250th anniversary of
his birth and the 200th anniversary of the publication of his *Rasselas,*
the Pierpont Morgan Library borrowed from two other institutions and
eleven private collectors in California, Connecticut, New Jersey, New
York, and Pennsylvania further to enrich its own fine resources. The
catalog of this memorable exhibition, published by the Morgan Library
in 1959, described a mass of manuscript material and many of the
rarest printed items now owned by libraries and collectors in this
country.

It would be impossible to overestimate the valuable service performed by the officials of the Walters Art Gallery and by Miss Dorothy
E. Miner, its librarian, in assembling its large, representative exhibitions of *Illuminated Books of the Middle Ages and Renaissance* (1949)
and, more recently, *The History of Bookbinding* (1957). These magnificent records of our civilization put us forever in the debt of those who
have performed the arduous task of collecting examples from many
collections in this country, and arranging and describing them in
printed catalogs.

Exhibitions held in our great special libraries, such as the Morgan

Library, the Huntington, the John Carter Brown, and the William L. Clements, have been viewed and admired for many years. The exhibition of the treasures in these collections has been a recognized function of these libraries ever since they were opened to the public. The publications describing the exhibitions, ranging from the inexpensive hand lists of the Huntington Library on *Rare Newspapers* (1931), *Tudor Drama* (1932), *A Century of California Literature* (1950), and the like, to the *Catalogue of Central European Manuscripts in the Pierpont Morgan Library* recently published at a price to permit handsome illustrations, all have their reference value. In England, the John Rylands Library, of Manchester, has provided invaluable reference guides to the transmission of the Bible in the catalog of its series of Bible exhibitions ranging from that of 1925, commemorating the 400th anniversary of the publication of William Tyndale's first printed New Testament, 1525, to the catalog of the exhibition, concluded on March 31, 1962, which commemorated the 350th anniversary of the King James version of the Bible and presented the resources of one of the great collections of the world.

The circulation of materials from rare book and special collections is not customary and is undertaken only in a limited sense under very special conditions. It would be paradoxical, indeed, to circulate freely, like other books, the very books and manuscripts which have been selected carefully as worthy of special treatment under maximum security regulations to ensure their preservation. The use of these materials is necessarily restricted to the confines of the rare book room. This means that these materials are requested on call slips presented at the curator's desk, and after use the books are returned to that desk for examination. Such materials are not issued to any reader, or student, without calling his attention to the rules in force at the institution. Some collections may permit lending for exhibition purposes and occasionally for interlibrary loan or classroom or seminar room display, but practice varies and many libraries *do not lend under any circumstances*.

The most frequent circulation outside the domain of the rare book room or special collections department is for exhibition purposes. This is not a circulation in the ordinary sense, since it involves only transferring materials from one locked area to another. Usually an exhibition area is in a convenient location where visitors may see the display without going far out of their way. If the exhibition is in a large, cosmopolitan community, it may be necessary to have a guard or custodian on duty, not merely for security, but also for answering questions and distributing catalogs. Sometimes the rare books are sent to libraries for exhibition at places somewhat remote from the lending institution. The classic example of this, of course, was the tour of the treasures of the Morgan Library which were shown in various metropolitan areas in the Midwest, the Far West, and New England. This was accomplished in an ideal way and in keeping with the value and importance of the materials which were shown. Exhibition cases were sent along, and trained personnel qualified to handle these special items traveled with the exhibition to install it in each city where it was shown.

When books or manuscripts are requested for exhibition in another institution, the request must be scrutinized and considered from all points of view by the administrators of the lending institution. The location of the exhibition, its probable importance, the reputation of the personnel who will handle the materials are all important considerations, but perhaps most important of all is the condition of the items requested. Fragility of the item is the factor to be considered, as the possibility of physical damage to any rare book or manuscript may prevent its circulation under what might seem to be the most favorable conditions. Occasionally size and bulk may make a loan impractical. The method of transportation is an important consideration, as is the length of time the item will be away from the collection. Distance may not be a great problem, since materials must be very carefully packed for any journey, and once they are safely in their cases, they will travel across the country as easily as to a neighboring town.

The care and skill with which the packing is done are most important. "Jiffy" bags are never used, and pasteboard cartons are seldom adequate protection for rare books and manuscripts. Wooden cases with individual items sturdily wrapped in soft packing material are essential. One problem of packing an illuminated manuscript of large folio size, weighing nearly fifty pounds, was solved by an offer from the borrowing institution to construct a heavy wooden case made to measure. All objections to the loan were removed when the empty case arrived, complete with screws and proper braces to hold the book in place. Shipment may be made in several ways, but Railway Express is recommended by many institutions, and the insurance is easily handled when the institution operates with a Fine Arts Policy. It is important to notify the insurance company of the items and their value, the date of shipment, where they are to be located, and when they are to return.

The decision to lend locally is sometimes difficult to make, as this type of loan may involve considerable risk. Certain local groups may not understand security requirements and the responsibilities involved. In many cases the curator must make the decision and, if he is a person with tact, he can perhaps improve public relations rather than damage them by a careful explanation of the reasons why the public must come to the book rather than have the book go to a place where security measures are not adequate.

The system of interlibrary loan which has been so highly developed in American libraries during recent decades accounts for the circulation of books and manuscripts from special collections to only a limited degree. Here, again, the considered judgment of the curator may be the determining factor in reaching a decision to lend or not to lend. Some institutions are unable to lend under any circumstances due to stipulations in the deed of gift. Those who are not bound by these

conditions should exercise logical thinking, although some decisions
may not satisfy the eager or serious scholar whose request is denied.
Although the borrowing library agrees to impose the same conditions
for use as those observed at the home library, refusal may be made on
grounds of uniqueness, fragility, or excessive value. Theoretically, at
least, the risk may be no greater than the risk of lending for exhibition
away from home. Usually, a rare book must be carefully transported
from one rare book room to another, kept under lock and key, and used
only under supervision.

At some academic institutions certain books and other graphic materials in special collections may be removed from their permanent
quarters for display in the classroom or seminar room on special occasions. Perhaps this should remain the exception, even though requests may become more frequent. In such cases the curator may find
it necessary to exercise his ingenuity in convincing the professor that
the materials in his care may be irreplaceable, careful handling is required, and extensive physical use by large numbers of students forbidden. Professors may be persuaded to bring their classes to the
rare book room where the desired books and manuscripts will be properly displayed and, on occasion, may be handled at the discretion of the
curator or the assistant in charge. There may be times when the professor may be a difficult person to convince, but an understanding one
will accept the curator's suggestions with grace.

The late Randolph G. Adams has written: "Rare books must be
segregated as much to defend them from the assaults of ignorant professors as to protect them against careless readers."[5] In the few
cases when it may seem advisable to send books to the classroom or
seminar room, they should be in the custody of the curator or his assistant in the department of special collections, who will supervise
their use.

PUBLICATIONS

Rare book collections are often known by their publications. Consequently it is important to promote each publication according to some
specific program and to plan the format in relation to its purpose and
eventual recipients. Such publications will be descriptive in nature although they will vary in method of presentation. Some will be designed
primarily as aids to scholarship, but all of them will serve as publicity.
They should be attractive in appearance if they are to be deserving of
attention. The distribution of most publications should be a matter
carefully considered and not handled haphazardly without a clear plan
of operation.

The curator has a responsibility and an obligation to make his

---

[5] Randolph G. Adams, "Who Uses a Library of Rare Books?," *English Institute Annual, 1940* (New York: Columbia Univ. Pr., 1941), p.153; also, "Librarians as Enemies
of Books," *Library Quarterly,* 7:317 ff. (July 1937).

materials known, especially to his own institution, to Friends of the library and potential Friends, and to the world of scholarship. Librarians should assume direct responsibility for descriptive books or brochures about the collections or parts of them, for exhibition catalogs, and for annual reports. Indirectly the librarians should assume the responsibility for bibliographies and for printed catalogs. These may be prepared by scholars in special fields or a faculty member, oftentimes with the aid of the curator.

The descriptive book, brochure, or leaflet describing large collections, small groups of books, or single books, may serve many different purposes. These publications are relatively easy and inexpensive to produce, so it may be useful to treat them first. They help to publicize the collections for Friends and for potential donors, and to a much less extent (but not a negligible one) they will bring material to the attention of scholars. They may even arouse a latent interest in book collecting and focus the layman's attention on the world of books. An information leaflet serves so many purposes that its distribution should be rather general. It may be mailed to other libraries, on an exchange basis, and sent out to Friends. In large libraries it may be sold at a publications desk. Within the rare book room it may be useful to mail out in answer to inquiries by letter, or to hand out to the visitor as a guide to his visit.

The many possibilities of this type of publication seem not to have been realized. From its beginning the William L. Clements Library has had an extensive publishing program, and a file of its publications will illustrate the range that is possible for the large special library. The list of Clements publications includes books describing the laying of the cornerstone; the founder's own historical and informative books; books about papers included in the collection; facsimiles of important books, manuscripts, and maps; brochures describing the building and its contents; and publicity leaflets.

The publications of the Colby College Library are an example of what may be done in a smaller academic community. The Library, in Waterville, Maine, is fortunate in the variety of its publications, inaugurated by the enterprising Professor Carl J. Weber. Professor Weber, until 1958, was personally responsible for books and brochures relating to important collections in his care, with special attention to Maine authors. As an example there is *A Bibliography of the Published Writings of Sarah Orne Jewett,* compiled by Clara Carter Weber and Carl J. Weber and published by the college in 1949. The Colby College monographs include *Edwin Arlington Robinson and His Manuscripts,* by Esther W. Bates (1944), and an important exhibition catalog, *A Descriptive Catalogue of the Grolier Club Centenary Exhibition of the Works of Thomas Hardy (1940).* The *Colby Library Quarterly* is rich in descriptive notes, checklists of special author and printer collections, and publications from them. Among the authors represented are Henry James, A. E. Housman, and George William Russell, better known as A.E.

Reprints of periodical articles may serve as descriptions of collections. These are invariably addressed to the Friends of a given institution who have already signified interest in the rare book collections through financial support, gifts of books and manuscripts, or both. One noteworthy example is an article reprinted from the *Yale Alumni Magazine,* entitled, "The Rare Book Room of the Yale University Library." The text is brief but informative, with illustrations which show a number of the books and manuscripts in addition to pictures of the room and its users. On the back page, Librarian James T. Babb presents a statement about the Yale Library Associates. At Yale, as at many institutions, the Librarian serves as the Secretary of the Associates or Friends.

An article in the alumni magazine is one way of enlisting membership for this valuable organization, which often provides the chief financial support for a rare book collection. Those who become Associates or Friends usually receive a bulletin of some nature as well as the annual reports of the Library concerned. These bulletins may not be the direct responsibility of the librarians. Procedures are not common to many of these organizations, as individual groups set up their own regulations. But the librarians and curators are nearly always involved, in one way or another, in the publications of the Friends. At Wellesley, for instance, all bulletins of the Friends have been the direct responsibility of the Librarian and of the Research Librarian in Charge of Special Collections. Certain of these Wellesley bulletins have been monographs describing collections, and others have been catalogs of exhibitions. They are issued only occasionally.

Usually larger institutions issue their publications with greater regularity. The *Princeton University Library Chronicle* is issued quarterly under the editorship of Alexander Wainwright, a staff member. *Columbia Library Columns* is published three times a year by Columbia University. In each issue it contains notes on "Our Growing Collections," contributed by Roland Baughman, head of the Department of Special Collections, and describes the important gift collections received by that library. The *Library Chronicle* of the University of Pennsylvania is issued twice each year under the editorship of Rudolf Hirsch, the associate director of the library. In recent years many other institutions have been publishing such periodicals regularly: Yale, Cornell, Duke, Newberry Library, and the University of Miami, among others.

Printed catalogs and bibliographies of collections are the tools of librarians and scholars. They are costly and time-consuming to produce, but the world of scholarship could not function without them. They range in size and importance from the printed catalog of the John Carter Brown Library (1919-31, in five volumes) to the ten-page mimeographed checklist of *American Imprints before 1801 in the Libraries of Williams College Not in "Evans,"* issued in 1957. It is no longer usual to issue catalogs of entire libraries in book form because they are so quickly outmoded and the cost of reprinting is prohibitive. The

American library contribution of the card catalog has developed to such proportions, however, that it too presents its problems. There may, in fact, be a change back to the bound volume as an accepted form of catalog now that there are inexpensive forms of reproduction which do not require the usual mechanical type composition and normal printing procedures. In recent years we have experienced a noticeable increase in the publication of the card catalog in book form, reproduced from the actual typed cards prepared for the individual libraries. These are sometimes expensive to purchase, but many of the special holdings provide excellent reference tools for newer and less fortunate institutions who lack the original materials.

Catalogs of rare materials and of special collections do not lose their usefulness even when they are out of date. The two printed catalogs at Wellesley, *A Catalogue of Early and Rare Editions of English Poetry* and *The Catalogue of the Frances Taylor Pearsons Plimpton Collection of Italian Books and Manuscripts,* are used by scholars and dealers today, even though they were published in 1923 and in 1929, respectively, and have since been supplemented by sizable card files. The use of these two collections outside the campus is a result of the distribution of these catalogs in the libraries of this country and of Europe. The donors of the collections provided for the catalogs and for their distribution. Happily this procedure is still followed by some collectors today.

Checklists, catalogs, and bibliographies of single author collections or of collections on special subjects are more numerous and no less useful. They, too, are serious and costly undertakings which may take a lifetime to produce. The catalog of the Beinecke Stevenson Collection at Yale (five volumes, 1951-61), to be complete in six volumes, is a recent example of the catalog of a single author collection. A Browning Catalogue has been in progress at Wellesley for many years. The Browning bibliography, published by Cornell in 1953, was completed by Robert Pearsall after the deaths of Professors Broughton and Northup, who had devoted years of their lives in bringing this bibliography near to completion.

Exhibition catalogs serve useful purposes, which have already been referred to as a reference service. They serve as finding lists and also aid in publicizing a library. They may inform the mind as well as delight the eye. It is safe to say that exhibition catalogs are more widely distributed than any other type of library publication with the possible exception of the annual report.

The annual report is a summary of the year's events prepared as an official account, by the administrator of the special library or of special collections, to the governing body of the institution. It generally includes a record of important acquisitions, names of donors, services rendered, the number of scholars served, and the activities of the staff. The report, though it is directed to an official governing board, is often of interest and value to colleagues, to Friends, to bookdealers—in short, to bookmen everywhere.

The format of library publications deserves more attention than it
often receives. The humblest publication of the rare book collection—
mailing label or sheet of rules and regulations—should be designed in
good taste and attractively printed. The famous dictum of William
Morris, "Fitness to use," should be applied to all publications. Items
which are produced either primarily or incidentally for publicity particularly ought to be appropriately designed, well printed, with suitable
illustrations, and whenever possible printed by a qualified press or a
distinguished printer. Such publications may even be sought as collectors' items. The Clements Library publications deserve a place on
collectors' shelves, as do many of those from such libraries as Princeton, Morgan, Dartmouth, Texas, Houghton, Huntington, Colby, and California.

The cost of publications is always an important consideration and
may sometimes seem prohibitive. Good printing, however, is not necessarily more expensive than bad. One should strive for the best, and
take every precaution when dealing with firms that cannot provide the
best. If the Anthoensen Press or some other reliable printing firm is
available, the librarian who is in charge of publications may hand over
accurate copy confident that it will be designed and printed according
to high standards and achieve a satisfactory result. If the library must
deal with a local printer who has had little experience with the type of
publication needed, the curator may be required to assume the responsibility for the selection of paper and type face, as well as the design
and layout.

Because of the intricacies of design and the importance of accuracy,
orders for printed catalogs and bibliographies of collections published
in book form are usually placed with university presses or commercial
printers specializing in this type of scholarly work. The skilled labor
involved in preparing these publications does not allow the institution
to risk its reputation by using local job printers. Taste, as well as attention to quality, will determine the book's attractiveness, and many
scholarly presses are qualified to produce such books. George McKay,
compiler of the Beinecke Stevenson Catalogue, paid tribute to the late
Carl Purington Rollins, designer of that monumental edition, as a man
"who was most helpful in solving typographical problems." This catalog is proof of the importance of good design in this type of publication.
A skilled and reputable printer can solve many details for librarians
through the use of wise and economical methods gained from years of
experience.

Although exhibition catalogs are improved by illustrations, many
catalogs are not illustrated because of the high cost and the difficulty
in preparing the artwork. The Huntington Library benefits from the
work of a variety of fine printers on the West Coast, and the use of illustrations in its catalogs is generally noticed. One of the Huntington
exhibition catalogs, *Great Books in Great Editions,* was printed in 1954
by Anderson, Ritchie & Simon, and included a full complement of illustrative plates. There is a plate for each of the twenty-eight items, the

ultimate in illustrated catalogs, making it a very useful and attractive hand list. Few libraries can afford to indulge in such profuse illustration, however, and the smaller institution may find it adequate to issue a simple leaflet prepared by the local printer with a minimum of illustrations. An attractive hand list may be prepared by paying attention to quality of paper, proper type faces, and appropriate design, thus creating a list that is useful and inexpensive.

The annual report usually receives less attention as to appearance than does any other type of library publication. This is indubitably because it is considered in its first right only—as a business document. We have already observed that such reports are widely distributed, however, and greatly prized in book circles. Surely, the annual report deserves more than mere clarity of presentation. Granted that letter-press is now considered expensive, offset printing may be used if it is done by quality printers, but mimeographing seldom fulfills the requisites of clarity and neat appearance. The annual report, as well as any other publication dealing with rare and special materials, should be presented in a form worthy of its subject matter. Although one library's mimeographed monstrosity represents hundreds of hours of labor, it is not likely to be bound and preserved for rereading and reference, whereas the attractive and well-printed "Reports" from Morgan, Houghton, and certain other rare book libraries will always occupy preferred space in any library where the curator is a true professional.

Chapter X

The Rare Book Library and the Public

JOHN PARKER

There is probably no part of a library's holdings that is less known and understood by library patrons and the general public than the rare materials. The very restrictions normally placed upon their use makes this inevitable. Yet there are no materials more likely to be used in a library's public relations program than rare books and manuscripts. This is presumably true because current books, magazines, newspapers, and journals are so taken for granted that only the unusual, the exotic, or the unique library material is likely to be considered newsworthy.

It is futile for the rare book librarian to ponder the merits of informing the general public about his holdings. He may believe in spending his time building the better mousetrap, but his director is likely to believe in public relations. Colleges, universities, and public libraries have departments and officials whose responsibility it is to publicize their institutions. The rare book librarian will be called upon—and frequently. He must be prepared to do his part.

The term "public relations" to some is an odious one, implying an approach that produces a somewhat less than true or an unduly magnified picture of the subject treated. It suggests advertising, which some of us might not consider a pursuit worthy of a librarian. The relationship of the rare book collection to the public need not be on anything but the highest level of honesty and integrity, for this will produce the best possible public relations. Books in their natural state are interesting to people, and have been for centuries. They can be publicized for their true literary, historical, artistic, or other merit, and can thereby strike responsive intellectual and emotional notes among the public. Doing the books justice is itself a real challenge.

Because the rare book librarian, more than any other person on the library staff, is likely to know the true merits of the books he keeps, he is the best person to handle publicity involving rare materials. He cannot prevent newswriters from choosing an angle to develop which may not be the major importance of the book, but he is the source of information and should try to make the true importance of the book sufficiently interesting to capture the interest of the professional publicity agent.

The public exhibit is, of course, the traditional way to show the public what types of materials are in the collection, and also to call attention to particular items. Yet, before treating exhibits in detail, it is worthwhile to consider other major media of publicity. The public gets more of its information on all subjects by way of newspapers, magazines, television, and radio. Each of these affords a means of developing and sustaining a public interest in a rare book collection.

Of the two hundred and more pounds of newsprint used by each person in the United States annually, somewhat less than an ounce, probably, is given to publicizing rare books. Yet newspapers and magazines do present an opportunity to inform a great number of people on this subject. Despite the abundance in the daily paper of what appears to be trivia, it is not easy to get a story on rare books placed prominently in the news. There are some civic-minded publishers who are pleased to call attention to cultural matters of this type, but others will ask what reader interest they have, and it is probably true that nothing short of a major book theft would attract the average reader.

It is necessary for the rare book librarian who wishes to inform the public through the newspaper to have as close a relationship as possible with a reporter for the local daily paper, or a connection with the editor of the book page. He must expect his stories to be trimmed and altered even after he has seen the reporter's copy, and the headline may emphasize an angle that attracted the reporter but is of minor significance in the true importance of the book. Yet it is publicity, and must be considered better than none.

Publicity in magazines is more difficult to achieve, yet because of greater planning time available, a rather complete story is more possible. Magazines of a topical interest lend themselves to accounts of unique and unusual material in their field. Again, the bookman must reconcile himself to seeing the story appear under the name of one who is less expert, perhaps, than would be wished. Such publicity, while confined to subscribers, is however frequently national in scope.

Television for educational purposes is still in its infancy. As a part of an educational institution, rare book departments may for the first time reach the homes of people who were uninformed or even unaware of them. Television also provides an opportunity for interested people to see more of a book than can be shown in an exhibit: pages can be turned, illustrations compared, the contents of the book shown in detail. As institutions develop their educational television programs, the rare book librarian has an outstanding opportunity to gain attention for his materials, and he must not feel limited to the traditional forms of exhibit.

While radio lacks the visual appeal of television, it presents an opportunity for description and discussion for the benefit of the person

out of range of his television set. A skillful interviewer can bring out
the information which the public will find interesting. Rare book librarians in colleges and universities may find an opportunity for this
type of publicity through the institution's radio station.

Finally, there is the personal appearance of the librarian as a
speaker, which enables him to learn directly what aspects of his collection have the greatest public appeal. Most communities have organizations which seek speakers on subjects of intellectual interest. A
rare book librarian can bring them a program based upon little-known
sources, and be both informative and entertaining. In seeking publicity
for his library he should see to it that his name comes to the attention
of one or two such organizations. If the program has popular interest,
word of it will travel fast, and as a result a large number of people can
be given an opportunity to inform themselves through question-and-
answer sessions that frequently follow such programs.

These media are mentioned here as devices by which the rare book
librarian can call attention to the public that his library exists. If he
does so successfully, he not only will have a community that is generally aware of the library, but will develop a curiosity and a continuing
interest among some members of that public who for one reason or another will want to know more about his collection of rare books.

FRIENDS OF THE LIBRARY

It is among such bookish people as these, who are not contented with
the mere awareness of the existence of the rare book collection, that
the possibility lies for organizing a group of intellectual and financial
supporters of the library which can be known by the general term,
"Friends of the Library." Such groups exist with relationship to libraries of all types, and their existence can be beneficial to both the
library and the membership.

The two motives from which such organizations are likely to spring
are the desire to stimulate a greater interest in the collection through
programs of education and information and the desire to raise money
for the support of the collection. The two motives will probably never
be distinctly separate, but one of them is almost certain to dominate,
and the librarian can determine which is to be the primary motive in
the organization with which he is associated. Members may join for
one motive or the other, but it is essential for the success of the organization that the librarian admit frankly, to himself at least, what the
aims of the group are.

The community in which the library is located will be a factor worth
studying to determine the course the organization should take, for the
appeal of the collection will vary with its identity with the community in
which it is located, and with its identity with certain groups in the community. A collection of local and state history might have great popular
interest, but persons most able to contribute might be much more interested in a collection relating to the major industry of the area. A

collection based upon the gift of an individual donor may have great public appeal, but bibliophiles in the vicinity may take little interest in it.

If the librarian has determined that his Friends group exists for the purpose of building up a small bibliographic society interested in books—their physical nature and their content—he will approach persons for membership who have bibliographic interests, regardless of what they might be able to do toward financial support of the collection. In such a society millionaires may rub elbows with postal clerks, for income and occupation often bear no great influence on the bookishness of the individual. If contributions, other than nominal dues, are not solicited by the organization, a spirit of equality and harmony is likely to prevail, for all members will have the most basic common ground—an interest in the collection from the bibliographic point of view.

An organization of this type has little prestige value and may sustain itself on sheer book interest. The librarian, however, is in a position to make meetings interesting through relating the collection to the group, and if the giving of information is his motive for developing the organization, he ought to do so to the best of his ability and as frequently as the group requires. This exchange of the barest essentials, information for enthusiasm, may be modified by an assessment of dues to provide an occasional program involving expenditure, or a publications program to give the membership some tangible reflection of their interest. For example, a small dues assessment might provide an annual lecture by an authority on some of the materials in the collection. Or the income could be used to publish a facsimile, a translation, or some other edition of an item in the collection.

Whatever might be asked or given by the librarian, it is his duty, if a popular interest has been shown, to stimulate it further, or sustain it at least. This can be done only by a systematized program on which the group can count; even if it is only an annual meeting, it ought to be something the membership can look forward to. Probably nothing is more appreciated by booklovers than an exhibition of recent acquisitions. Not only does it give them a chance to see rare books, but it also gives them a sense of being informed about what directions the library is taking in its development. Along with an exhibit of the materials, the librarian should explain the significance of some of the items at least, for bookish people delight in knowing the points of interest in books even though they belong to someone else.

If possible, an exhibit with a speaker who is not a member of the group is most appropriate. This brings in new information, and if the speaker is a recognized authority, he lends distinction to the organization and to the library. If an exhibit for the general public is being planned, a preview for members is usually satisfactory to all concerned, for in addition to pleasing the membership, it puts the best information about the exhibit in the hands of those most likely to spread the news of it.

In planning programs of an informative nature, the librarian will do well to consider the most basic interest likely to be found in the organization. People love books for a variety of reasons, but in an average group only a small minority will get excited over small points of bibliographic detail, such as variants and typographic peculiarities. The content of the book and its historical significance are the features most likely to hold the attention of the group. Typographic and illustrative materials are also points of considerable interest, especially if they can be exhibited well. If information is the motive for the organization's existence, it should be tailored to the general level of the group's understanding. Improvement of the members' bibliographic knowledge will come out of their enthusiasm. A librarian who talks over their heads merely because he can does not bind his organization more closely to his library. He merely emphasizes the distance between them.

The administration of a Friends group of this type need not be complex. Perhaps the first point to be determined is whether or not dues are to be charged. If so, they should be sufficiently low so as not to exclude book-minded people of limited means, and these are many. It is likely that dues of even the most nominal amount will have some limiting effect on membership. It should be borne in mind, also, that the annual reminder for payment of dues imposes further administrative duties on the librarian, and renders the mailing list obsolete with each year's response. If no dues are assessed, the mailing list can grow to senseless proportions by a show of interest by a great many people who actually will participate little or not at all. Weeding out these dormant members always carries the danger of offending someone who wishes to continue as a member and whose dormancy may have been well justified. The mailing list should be kept manageable, and before removing names from it a special reminder should be sent to the member who has not participated or shown any interest for some time.

The structure of such an organization need not be complicated, but should be as simple as possible. If a president is named from among the membership, the librarian is under some obligation to consult with him on programs and other activities. The greater efficiency that might result from the librarian's direction of the group himself may be somewhat offset by the possibility of his being less in touch with the wishes of the members than a president might be. A constitution seems unnecessary for an organization of this type, and the reading of minutes or reports is likely to be a bore to people who attend meetings to learn about books. A formal statement of aims and purposes, however, as many librarians have discovered, is usually desirable, whether it is in a formal constitution or some other official document.

If dues have been paid, it will be natural for members to express themselves on the use of these funds for programs or other activities. In this the librarian will do well to conform to the group's wishes, although he is in a position to suggest speakers and publications from which they might choose.

There is, of course, nothing to prevent members of a Friends group, organized for education and information, from taking a financial interest in the collection and raising money for the purchase of books. Even if some substantial gifts do come in through the organization, the librarian should consider information his first purpose, unless he decides that it will be more beneficial to the library to place the emphasis on raising money. If the decision is made that the raising of money is the primary purpose of the group at its inception, a somewhat different type of organization will develop. If it is made after some experiment with the other motive, certain alterations in appeal, program, and administration will be required.

A Friends organization which has as its major interest the raising of funds will present the librarian with a more difficult task, for sharing information is considerably easier than asking others to share expenses. The literature of librarianship presents numerous instances where Friends groups have produced much needed funds for improvements, special projects, and improved book budgets in public libraries. Also, the annual reports of major rare book libraries show the financial strength they derive from their Friends.

The rare book librarians for whom these pages are intended, however, are those who will develop the less-known collections which have not the appeal of a John Carter Brown Library, and whose materials have not the wide appeal of a public library which provides the public with literature of all types in their own homes. These are limitations of which the librarian should be aware, yet they do not alter the fact that, in most communities where libraries and other institutions of learning exist, there will be people who are willing and eager to help support a rare book collection with their gifts.

Obviously, the search for membership will go beyond those who are merely interested in books, although the bibliophile with limited means should by all means be included. Beyond the book-minded citizenry are people with a strong sense of civic pride and responsibility who recognize libraries along with art galleries, museums, and symphony orchestras as cultural assets in their community, although they may have little interest in rare books themselves. Their concerns and contributions could aid the rare book collection and should not be spurned because they did not grow from a devout bibliographic interest. There are also organizations which concern themselves with aiding cultural institutions in the community, and these afford the librarian an opportunity to seek either the support of the organization or that of its interested members.

In many cities one may also find individuals who willingly spend their leisure time and their energy raising money for one worthy cause or another. These are worth seeking out, for their experience has probably taught them which citizens of the community can be counted on for support of organizations such as libraries. Finally, there is the person who is both public-spirited and a bibliophile, who can be approached with the confidence that the rare book collection will interest him at two levels, and that he will find satisfaction of a deeper variety in giving to help develop the library than will other donors.

To attract funds from any of these sources, the librarian must show that the collection is deserving of support. Few persons are donors to unknown causes. Upon organization of the Friends of the Library the librarian should prepare a statement describing the collection in brief, its major emphasis, its history, and plans for its future. Prospective members can thereby be informed of the true nature of the institution they are being asked to support, and to this they are entitled. This announcement should also state what dues are required for membership, and it should describe in a general way what programs are to be undertaken by the organization. In this way the prospective member can begin to see what benefits he might receive from the organization other than some knowledge of rare books.

This raises the question, what *can* the Friends organization offer the person whose major reason for joining is not bibliographic interest? Perhaps the most elementary benefit is publicity. An annual listing of membership in a report is gratifying to a number of people. The type of program offered can be an attraction if it is keyed to the type of people to whom the appeal is being made. It will be impossible to please everyone in this respect, for a supporter of cultural organizations will expect the library to produce a cultural program, whereas the professional joiner might prefer an exclusive cocktail party. The nature of the community is again worth considering, for an isolated area might look upon a lecture by an eminent authority as a great attraction, while a cosmopolitan city, where lectures of this kind are common, might prefer a private exhibit of recent gifts to the collection. Whatever the event, it should be publicized as well as possible, for few people are not impressed by having their names or their organizations noted in the newspapers.

In addition to publicity and a program to call attention to the group, the use of publications as annual remembrances is a good way to remind the members that they are getting something out of the organization. An item "For the Friends of the Library," published from the collection in an edition just equal to the number of members, carries the impression that this is a rather special organization.

If these various devices to attract the interest of persons who may be basically nonbookish seem to the librarian an imposition upon his time and talents as a bookman, he must reflect again on the purpose of it all. He is asking for money, and he represents one of many legitimate and worthwhile cultural and civic enterprises that compete for private funds. If those funds can be obtained without any of these activities, the latter might properly be dispensed with, for they are great time-consumers. An observation of the methods of other organizations competing for private funds leaves doubt that nonbookish people will join an organization for the support of a rare book library without some of these compensations. And forming the organization is only the beginning. The actual raising of funds beyond the dues paid for membership

is the purpose of its existence, and methods for doing this will have to
be worked out by the librarian in conjunction with the organization.

There may be members who can be approached directly for funds
to purchase a particular item, and the librarian will learn of this by
noting evidences of such generosity by the member toward other organizations. Presumably the President of the Friends would know which
members were willing to make such gifts, and he would be the logical
person to approach potential donors on specific purchases. The policy
of receiving memorials from members upon the death of friends or
relatives is a program of dignified and lasting remembrance. The
"book a year" idea, whereby each member would buy one item, has the
merit of developing interest and pride in the items gathered by each
member for the library, yet it could offend those incapable of anything
but the smallest purchases. A book sale at which members turned over
unwanted private books for sale to the public would yield some funds
for the group as a whole.

It is possible to raise money out of proportion to the number of
members if various types of memberships are established, such as ordinary, contributing, and sustaining memberships. These afford the
means of getting substantial sums from members through the annual
canvass, and may make the occasional approach for a gift less necessary.

The administration of a Friends organization for the purpose of
raising funds will require time and discretion in abundance. There are
no simple or scientific answers to the problems that can arise. Most
people in the library profession are not sufficiently wealthy to belong
to the group that is looked to most frequently for funds for purposes of
this type. Hence, the librarian is required to appeal to people with
whom he does not regularly associate. A sense of civic responsibility
does not make a bookman out of a banker, yet the feeling of civic responsibility may induce the banker to help build a library. A problem
arises if his financial interest leads him to assume the right to advise
on acquisitions policy, or the right to request an exhibit of books at a
meeting of some other organization, such as Rotary. Such problems
are not inevitable, but they have arisen in fund-raising organizations.

The genuine bibliophile who wishes to present books to the collection that are outside the scope of the collection presents another problem for which there is no standard answer. A sacrifice of principle
for the time being may bring good results, or it may merely clutter up
the library with items to be apologized for. The less generous bibliophile, who merely advises that the library purchase certain items,
must be controlled in his willingness to spend the librarian's book budget, but again it should be done without offending him. The problem of
what to do about the person who does not pay his dues is not always
easy to solve. He may have merely forgotten, or he may have been
away at the time of the last mailing. He may be the person most frequently willing to buy an item for the library when the book budget is
depleted. Some more positive evidence of decline in interest than

nonpayment of dues should be required before taking him off the mailing list.

A part of the administration of a Friends organization is that of keeping a membership list, and keeping it with sufficient care so that members who have moved, lost interest, or died are not sent mailings. Another record that should be kept with care is a record of gifts. It is not uncommon for a donor to drop in to see a book bought with his money or wish to show it to a friend. He will not understand why the librarian does not recall which book it was, and the inability to find it promptly may indicate to him a lack of respect for the gift.

Administration of this type of organization will require a more elaborate structure than that of a bibliographic society. The greater prestige of a fund-raising group will make its offices attractive to some, and the handling of money will require a responsible administration. A constitution is commonly a feature of organizations with social status. In this structure the librarian should find a position of an advisory nature which is permanent, for he is the link between the library and the organization. Whatever his position, it is essential that he control acquisitions policy and publicity, for the library and its public reputation are dependent upon these aspects of its administration.

As most rare book libraries are a part of larger libraries, it is likely that any Friends group affiliated with the former will have some relationship with the latter. In this situation the librarian will probably not be an entirely free agent in setting up his organization or working with it, but he is almost certain to be instrumental in its functions if the director of the library wishes to focus interest of the Friends on the rare book collection. It is certain that he will be the key person in relating the books to the organization, and one of the best ways of doing this is an exhibit.

PREPARING EXHIBITS

"Of all the things a rare book library can do, this is the best, for you show us what you have." This was the appraisal of exhibits made to the writer by an outstanding collector. The exhibit is the traditional way of sharing with the public books which cannot be taken home to read or which require interpretation by one who knows their true merit. The preparation of an exhibit is, therefore, a responsibility not unlike the writing of a book, for it will communicate all that many will ever know about certain items in the library.

A good exhibit will be prepared only with the realization of the major purpose of exhibits—the communication of information. To do this successfully the librarian must have clearly in mind what he wants to pass on to his public, and all aspects of the exhibit must bear upon that subject. It may be that the exhibit is to show gifts to the library by members of the Friends of the Library. The nature of a complete exhibit requires that all items must then be of this same origin. If the exhibit is to tell a story, then it must have a beginning and an end, and every item in the exhibit must contribute something to that story. Whatever the dominant theme, the exhibit must be unified in the materials it presents, and it acquires unity by the proper relation of items in the exhibit.

This does not mean that if a library has exhibit space for sixty books, the librarian must wait for sixty gifts in order to make a public exhibit. The cases can be grouped so as to make possible two or three exhibits at once, but the different exhibits should be clearly defined. Or the cases can feature the first editions of books from the rare book collection if they are gifts, and show later editions from the general library, making it clear which is the most important book in each case. If the exhibit is to include recent acquisitions, they should be grouped in some logical way, such as subject, language, or donor, so that each book relates to some other item in the case.

The exhibit which tells a story is one which attracts attention readily. If it is well prepared, there will be numerous opportunities for comparison of book manufacture, technique of illustration, and early and later portrayals of the subject. The mapping of a region, the history of costume in the life of a city, the history of printing or engraving, and other subjects of this type can be made into interesting stories which are extremely informative if authentically done and if each item is made to do its part by being different from every other item, yet a part of the continuous narrative.

Authentication can be achieved only by careful thought and sometimes considerable research. Haste in preparation will invariably produce embarrassment when some expert calls attention to the exhibitor's errors, just as many people find mistakes in supposedly accurate books. Some errors of fact in the treatment of subject matter are to be expected, although these are less likely when the subject is the special interest of the librarian. Certain mistakes in relationship between items exhibited are unforgivable. One ought not to include a steamship model in an exhibit of eighteenth-century books on ship design, or show eighteenth-century costumes in a centennial exhibit.

When a subject for the exhibit has been chosen, books should be selected for the contribution they can make to the total exhibit. There should be a balance between illustrative material, title pages, and text in the selection of pages to be shown. The illustrations should be pertinent rather than merely appealing, and a page of text can be as interesting as an engraving if it is selected with care. Title pages with picturesque language from the past can be very attractive, and so may even the spine of a book, when the title on it is informative. To get the greatest utility out of an exhibit of books in several languages, those in the less-frequently-read languages should be opened to illustrative material; French, German, and Spanish titles can be read by a considerable number of viewers; and a page of text will naturally get its widest reading in the English language.

At the time a book is selected for the exhibit, the pages to be shown should be decided upon. When a sufficient number of books has been selected for one phase of the exhibit, annotations should be prepared. In this way the annotations will properly show greater unity in their treatment of the subject than if no particular order of work is followed. Annotations are a very important part of the exhibit, for the few words written about each book explain its significance. And the words should be few. Annotation cards measuring three inches by five inches are sufficiently large if a regular typewriter is used, and they should give information as to the author, title, and publisher followed by from four to six lines of description of the book as it pertains to the particular exhibit.

Unifying the annotations is made easier if the exhibit case contains one general annotation made with poster type or any of the art letters commercially available. A placard, such as one announcing "Early Explorers of the Rockies," gives each annotation card an assist in putting across its message. The annotations should be typed neatly and by an expert. They should be proofread with great care, for every error will be found by the public if the exhibit remains on view for any length of time.

Assuming that the exhibit cases are empty when the new exhibit is begun—and they should be to avoid the puzzled looks if, for instance, rare medical books were to appear next to children's literature—they should be completed one at a time, if possible. A case full of books without annotations will leave viewers with questions to ask; if they do not ask them, they may go away with no information at all. The actual preparation of the books will present a number of physical problems, for some will not stand up gracefully and others will refuse to remain open when lying flat unless some device is used to hold them thus. Books can be held open by tying them with vertical thin strips of clear acetate. The ends of these strips can be joined at the back by stapling them to cardboard strips, by tying them, or by using clear adhesive tape. Clear acetate has no harmful chemical content and is transparent so that nothing of the page is hidden due to its use.

Books that will not remain open even with one strip of this material on either side can be helped by joining the two vertical strips with a stiff horizontal cardboard strip at the back, although great care must be taken not to attempt to force the book to open too wide. Narrow ribbon can also be used to tie pages open but not rubber bands because their chemical content will discolor pages. Likewise, paper clips should never be used.

The books should be placed at a variety of angles in a vertical case. Some will appear well lying flat, while others can be propped up slightly with small wooden blocks. A pleasant angle for viewing can be achieved through the use of plastic or wire stands that are commercially available.

Whether cases are large or small, horizontal or vertical, they should have a background that is distinctive. A very small case with a black background shows off a page of type to good advantage, but larger cases need more brilliant colors. In most exhibit cases it is possible to change the background color by inserting various types of art board. Ideally, the background will consist of more than a colored surface, especially in vertical cases. Maps, engravings, quotations, prints, all give content to the background, but they should be annotated just as the books are, with the annotation mounted below or to one side of the item. Frequently the background can include a design which ties the whole exhibit together, such as a state emblem for an exhibit of materials pertaining to the history of the state.

The background can effectively include aids to the understanding of the subject, such as hand-drawn maps, pictures, and the like, but these should be simple and functional—supplementing the material being exhibited without any attempt to dominate the exhibit case. Any artistic aids that are employed should follow the same general rule.

An exhibit should be well lighted, but care must be taken that the lights do not give off so much heat as to dry out bindings and warp the covers of books. Most modern exhibit cases are built with this precaution in mind. The exhibit case without lights should be placed in a well-lighted location, whether the light be artificial or natural, but not in a position that permits direct sunlight to shine on the materials. The placement of a library building, the lighting facilities available, and the ingenuity of the librarian make the problem of lighting highly individualistic. If there is a rule of thumb, it is simply this—the finest print on the annotation cards should be easy to read.

Taking books out of a vault and placing them in exhibit cases in a corridor, just inches from the hands of the public, naturally involves some security risk. No one can predict which person might covet one of the books enough to attempt to take it from the case. The theft of a book is the least desirable publicity a library can receive. Despite this ever present risk, exhibits of rare books are constantly being held, and the theft of a book from an exhibit is rare indeed.[1] Exhibit cases must be securely locked at all times as the most basic precaution, and, if possible, safety devices requiring special tools to open them are advisable. Again there is no neat rule to follow for the safeguarding of books. The librarian must weigh the cost and possibility of replacement of an item against the security the exhibit cases afford. The books, after all, are his responsibility.

All of the above has been written with the exhibit of books belonging to a particular library in mind. It is possible to create exhibits from materials in part or entirely on loan from other libraries. A library which values its rare books will not send them out without knowing in detail the nature of the exhibit, its duration, the person responsible for it, the security afforded, and the means of getting the books to and from the borrowing institution. An exhibit can frequently be improved by materials on loan, but the borrowing librarian must ask the same questions of his library that he asks of others when a colleague requests books from him.

---

[1] Several instances were mentioned by Hannah French in Chapter IX, p. 94.

How long should an exhibit remain on view? The public may never tire of a good one, but there are other factors to consider, chiefly the preservation of the books, or possibly the need of the exhibit cases by other departments of the library. A month to six weeks would seem adequate for interested people to see the exhibit if it is well publicized. Despite the necessity for exhibits to end, and it is always a sad occasion when old books that have attracted an audience are put away, the exhibit can continue to live through the preparation of a catalog of it. This can be as simple or elaborate as funds permit. In any event, there should be a complete catalog of the exhibit in the librarian's files, including a case by case record of the books, annotations, artistic devices, lettering, and so on. This can be compiled from the annotation cards and other material as the exhibit is being installed or taken down.

A catalog of an exhibit—published and mailed to members of the Friends of the Library, to other libraries, and to book collectors—is one of the most traditional and dignified forms of publicity a rare book library can expect. It becomes then a traveling exhibit, and a permanent one. Such a catalog should contain a preface stating the dominant theme of the exhibit, the cover perhaps bearing some design from the exhibit, or at least the title of it. If the various cases had subtitles, the books should be arranged under these, and in any event should be arranged as they were in the exhibit. An exhibit catalog can be useful without containing reproductions, although most catalogs are enhanced by having several illustrations. Annotations can be expanded slightly to give some account of the physical book. If reproductions can be made, it is unlikely that all books in the exhibit would be reproduced. It would be best to choose key items from each case, especially those with attractive title pages or interesting illustrations.

The exhibit catalog becomes a reference book. To bookmen the catalog tells a story just as the exhibit does. It becomes a part of the program of integrating the work of an artist with that of a subject specialist and a storyteller. The rare book librarian has to be all of these to create a successful exhibit. Few libraries have full-time exhibits personnel, and even those that have, cannot expect such personnel fully to understand the content or tell the story the librarian feels in his rare book exhibit. The librarian may at best count upon the assistance of an artist, but he has no handy set of rules like the cataloger. Nor will he find very much helpful literature on the subject. In writing of exhibits, an anonymous librarian once said, "The essence of the work is the spirit of adventure," and this spirit alone makes it a rewarding work.

Appendix

A STATEMENT OF RECOMMENDED LIBRARY POLICY
REGARDING APPRAISALS

1. The appraising of a gift to a library for inheritance or tax purposes is the responsibility of the donor since it is the donor who requires an appraisal, not the library, but the library may make arrangements for and suggestions concerning appraisals.

2. The library should at all times protect the interests of its donors as best it can and should suggest the desirability of appraisals whenever such a suggestion would be in order.

3. To protect both its donors and itself, the library, as an interested party, should not appraise gifts made to it, except in those cases where only items of comparatively low monetary value are involved.

4. The acceptance of a gift which has been appraised by a third—and disinterested—party does not in any way imply an endorsement of the appraisal by the library.

5. The cost of the appraisal (if there is one) should ordinarily be borne by the donor.

6. The library should not appraise items for a private owner. It should limit its assistance to referring him to such sources as auction records and dealers' catalogs and to suggesting the names of appropriate commercial experts who might be consulted.

7. A librarian, if he is conscious that as an expert he may have to prove his competence in court, may properly act as an independent appraiser of library materials. He should not in any way suggest that his appraisal is endorsed by his library (such as by the use of the library's letterhead).

> Respectfully submitted,
>
> ACRL Rare Books Section
> Committee on Appraisals
> Alexander Wainwright, Chairman
> Stanley Pargellis
> John Cook Wyllie

Revised and approved by Membership
at Oberlin College: 7 July 1961

A Selected Bibliography

The following selected bibliography presents a listing of books, articles, and journals which the Editor believes will be useful to students and librarians interested in the topics covered by the various contributors to this book. To aid the user in finding the necessary references relating to particular matters without perusing the entire list, the entries have been arranged in four categories: Bibliographical Cataloging and Description; Conservation and Repair of Materials; Book Collecting, Including History of Books and Printing; and Miscellaneous References on Rare Book Libraries. It should be unnecessary to add that these categories are not mutually exclusive, but that some of the more comprehensive volumes overlap in other areas.

BIBLIOGRAPHICAL CATALOGING AND DESCRIPTION

Bowers, Fredson Thayer. *Principles of Bibliographical Description.* Princeton, N.J.: Princeton Univ. Pr., 1949.

Bühler, Curt Ferdinand, and others. *Standards of Bibliographical Description.* Philadelphia: Univ. of Pennsylvania Pr., 1949.

Cowley, John Duncan. *Bibliographical Description and Cataloging ...* London: Grafton, 1949.

Dunkin, Paul Shaner. *How To Catalog a Rare Book.* Chicago: American Library Association, 1951.

Esdaile, Arundell James Kennedy. *A Student's Manual of Bibliography.* 3d rev. ed.; rev. by Roy Stokes. London: Allen & Unwin, 1954.

McKerrow, Ronald Brunlees. *An Introduction to Bibliography for Literary Students.* Oxford, Eng.: Clarendon Pr., 1927.

Mann, Margaret. *Introduction to Cataloging and the Classification of Books.* 2d ed. Chicago: American Library Association, 1943.

Peckham, Howard H. "Arranging and Cataloguing Manuscripts in the William L. Clements Library," *American Archivist,* 1:215-29 (Oct. 1938).

Schneider, Georg. *Handbuch der Bibliographie.* Leipzig: Hiersemann, 1923. English translation of the 3d ed. by Ralph Robert Shaw. *Theory and History of Bibliography.* New York: Columbia Univ. Pr., 1934.

Willoughby, Edwin Eliott. *The Uses of Bibliography to the Students of Literature and History.* Hamden, Conn.: Shoe String, 1957.

Wilson, William Jerome. "Manuscript Cataloging." New York: Fordham Univ. Pr., 1956. An offprint from *Traditio*, 12:457-555 (1956).

CONSERVATION AND REPAIR OF MATERIALS

Barrow, William J. *Manuscripts and Documents, Their Deterioration and Restoration.* Charlottesville, Va.: Univ. of Virginia Pr., [1955].

Barrow (W. J.) Research Laboratory. *Permanence / Durability of the Book: A Two-Year Research Program.* [I]-III. Richmond, Va.: 1963-64.

Blades, William. *The Enemies of Books;* with a Preface by Richard Garnett. London: Elliot Stock, 1896.

Cockerell, Douglas. *Bookbinding, and the Care of Books: A Textbook for Bookbinders and Librarians.* 5th ed. London: Pitman, [1955]. ("Artistic Crafts Series of Technical Handbooks," [no.1])

Cockerell, Sydney M. *The Repairing of Books.* Illus. by Joan Rix Tebbutt. London: Sheppard Pr., [1958].

Grant, Julius. *Books & Documents: Dating, Permanence, and Preservation.* London: Grafton; New York: Chemical Pub. Co., 1937.

Grove, Lee E. "What Good Is Greenland?," *Wilson Library Bulletin,* 36:749-57 (May 1962).

The Lakeside Press, Chicago. *All the King's Horses and All the King's Men.* [Chicago: R. R. Donnelley, 1954]

Langwell, William Herbert. *The Conservation of Books and Documents;* with a Foreword by G. Barraclough. London: Pitman, [1957].

Lehmann-Haupt, Hellmut, ed. *Bookbinding in America; Three Essays:* Early American Bookbinding by Hand, by Hannah Dustin French... The Rise of American Edition Binding, by Joseph W. Rogers... On the Rebinding of Old Books, by Hellmut Lehmann-Haupt... Portland, Maine: Southworth-Anthoensen Pr., 1941.

Lydenberg, Harry Miller, and Archer, John. *The Care and Repair of Books.* 4th ed., rev. by John Alden. New York: Bowker, 1960.

Middleton, Bernard C. *A History of English Craft Bookbinding Technique.* New York: Hafner, [1963].

Plenderleith, Harold James. *The Conservation of Antiquities and Works of Art: Treatment, Repair, and Restoration.* London: Oxford Univ. Pr., [1956].

—— *The Preservation of Leather Bindings.* London: British Museum, [1947].

Tauber, Maurice F., ed. "Conservation of Library Materials," *Library Trends,* 4:213-334 (Jan. 1956).

Tribolet, Harold W. "Binding and Related Problems," *American Archivist*, 16:115-26 (April 1953).
—— "Trends in Preservation," *Library Trends*, 13:208-14 (Oct. 1964).
Virginia. State Library, Richmond. *Deterioration of Book Stock, Causes and Remedies. Two Studies on the Permanence of Book Paper Conducted by W. J. Barrow;* ed. by Randolph W. Church. Richmond, 1960. (Publications, no.10)
—— *The Manufacture and Testing of Durable Book Papers. Based on the Investigations of W. J. Barrow;* ed. by Randolph W. Church. Richmond, 1960. (Publications, no.13)

BOOK COLLECTING, INCLUDING HISTORY OF BOOKS AND PRINTING

Adams, Randolph Greenfield. *The Whys and Wherefores of the William L. Clements Library: A Brief Essay on Book Collecting as a Fine Art.* 2d ed. Ann Arbor: Univ. of Michigan Pr., 1930.
Arnold, William Harris. *First Report of a Book-Collector; Comprising: A Brief Answer to the Frequent Question "Why First Editions?"* Jamaica, N.Y.: Marion Pr., 1897-1898.
Bennett, Whitman. *A Practical Guide to American Book Collecting (1663-1940).* New York: Bennett Book Studios, [1941].
Bigmore, Edward Clements. *A Bibliography of Printing, with Notes and Illustrations.* London: Quaritch, 1880-1886. 3v.
Blanck, Jacob Nathaniel. *Bibliography of American Literature* ... New Haven, Conn.: Yale Univ. Pr., 1955-1963. (v.1-4 have been published to date, Adams through Ingraham)
Book Collecting and Scholarship; essays by Theodore C. Blegen, James Ford Bell, Stanley Pargellis, Colton Storm, and Louis B. Wright. Minneapolis: Univ. of Minnesota Pr., 1954.
Book Collector; "incorporating Book Handbook." London: Queen Anne Pr., 1952 to date.
Bookman's Glossary. 4th ed., rev. and enl. by Mary C. Turner. New York: Bowker, 1961.
Brigham, Clarence Saunders. *Fifty Years of Collecting Americana for the Library of the American Antiquarian Society, 1908-1958.* Worcester, Mass.: [American Antiquarian Society], 1958.
Cannon, Carl Leslie. *American Book Collectors and Collecting from Colonial Times to the Present.* New York: Wilson, 1941.
Carter, John. *ABC for Book-Collectors.* [3d ed., rev.] London: Mercury Books, [1961].
—— *Books and Book-Collecting.* London: Hart-Davis, 1956.
—— *Taste and Technique in Book-Collecting: A Study of Recent Developments in Great Britain and the United States.* Cambridge, Eng.: University Pr., 1948. (Sandars Lectures in Bibliography for 1947)
—— and Graham Pollard. *An Enquiry into the Nature of Certain Nineteenth Century Pamphlets.* London: Constable, 1934.

Collison, Robert L. *Book Collecting: An Introduction to Modern Methods of Literary and Bibliographical Detection.* London: Benn, [1957].

The Dolphin: A Periodical for All People Who Find Pleasure in Fine Books. No.1-4, pt. 3; 1933-Spring 1941. New York: Limited Editions Club, 1933-41. 4 nos. in 6v.

Glaister, Geoffrey Ashall. *An Encyclopedia of the Book ... Including Illustrations and Translated Extracts from Grafisk Uppslagsbok ...* Cleveland: World, [1960]. Published in England as *Glossary of the Book,* by Allen & Unwin, 1960.

Hertzberger, Menno. *Dictionary for the Antiquarian Booktrade in French, English, German, Swedish, Danish, Italian, Spanish and Dutch.* Paris: Ligue Internationale de la Librairie Ancienne, 1956.

Howes, Wright. *U.S.IANA (1650-1950): A Selective Bibliography in Which Are Described 11,620 Uncommon and Significant Books Relating to the Continental Portion of the United States.* Rev. and enl. 2d ed. New York: Bowker for the Newberry Library, 1962.

Jackson, Holbrook. *The Anatomy of Bibliomania.* London: Soncino Pr., 1932.

Landau, Thomas, ed. *Encyclopaedia of Librarianship.* London: Bowes & Bowes, [1958].

Lehmann-Haupt, Hellmut. *The Book in America: A History of the Making and Selling of Books in the United States ... in Collaboration with Lawrence C. Wroth and Rollo G. Silver.* 2d [rev. and enl.] ed. New York: Bowker, 1951.

———— *One Hundred Books about Bookmaking: A Guide to the Study and Appreciation of Printing.* New York: Columbia Univ. Pr., 1949.

———— ed. "Current Trends in Antiquarian Books," *Library Trends,* 9:387-492 (April 1961).

Lenhart, John Mary. *Pre-Reformation Printed Books: A Study in Statistical and Applied Bibliography ...* New York: Joseph F. Wagner, [1935].

Lewis, Wilmarth Sheldon. *Collector's Progress.* New York: Knopf, 1951.

McKay, George Leslie. *American Book Auction Catalogues, 1713-1934; a union list ...* with an Introduction by Clarence S. Brigham. New York: New York Public Library, 1937.

Muir, Percival Horace. *Points, 1874-1930: Being Extracts from a Bibliographer's Note-Book ...* London: Constable, 1931.

———— *Points, Second Series, 1866-1934 ...* London: Constable; New York: Bowker, 1934.

Munby, Alan Noel Latimer. *The Dispersal of the Phillipps Library.* Cambridge, Eng.: University Pr., 1960. ("Phillipps Studies," no.5)

———— *The Formation of the Phillipps Library.* Cambridge, Eng.: University Pr., 1954-56. 2v. ("Phillipps Studies," no.3-4)

Partington, Wilfred George. *Forging Ahead: The True Story of the Upward Progress of Thomas James Wise, Prince of Book Collectors,*

Bibliographer Extraordinary and Otherwise. New York: Putnam, [1939].

—— *Thomas J. Wise in the Original Cloth: The Life and Record of the Forger of the Nineteenth-Century Pamphlets;* with an Appendix by George Bernard Shaw. London: R. Hale, [1947].

Peckham, Howard H., ed. "Rare Book Libraries and Collections," *Library Trends,* 5:417-500 (April 1957).

Pollard, Alfred William, and Redgrave, G. R. *A Short-Title Catalogue of Books Printed in England, Scotland, & Ireland and of English Books Printed Abroad, 1475-1640.* London: Bibliographical Society, 1926.

Powell, Lawrence Clark. *The Alchemy of Books.* Los Angeles: Ward Ritchie Pr., 1954.

Quaritch, Bernard, ed. *Contributions towards a Dictionary of English Book-Collectors, ... Some Foreign Collectors Whose Libraries Were Incorporated in English Collections or Whose Books Are Chiefly Met with in England* ... London: Quaritch, 1892-1921.

Ricci, Seymour de. *The Book Collector's Guide: A Practical Hand-Book of British and American Bibliography.* Philadelphia: Rosenbach Co., 1921.

—— *English Collectors of Books & Manuscripts (1530-1930) and Their Marks of Ownership.* Cambridge, Eng.: University Pr., 1930.

Stillwell, Margaret Bingham. *Incunabula and Americana, 1450-1800: A Key to Bibliographical Study.* New York: Columbia Univ. Pr., 1931.

Storm, Colton, and Peckham, Howard. *Invitation to Book Collecting, Its Pleasures and Practices, with Kindred Discussions of Manuscripts, Maps, and Prints.* New York: Bowker, 1947.

Targ, William, ed. *Carrousel for Bibliophiles: A Treasury of Tales, Narratives, Songs, Epigrams and Sundry Curious Studies Relating to a Noble Theme.* New York: Duschnes, 1947.

Taylor, Archer. *Book Catalogues: Their Varieties and Uses.* Chicago: Newberry Library, 1957.

—— *Renaissance Guides to Books: An Inventory and Some Conclusions.* Berkeley and Los Angeles: Univ. of California Pr., 1945.

Thompson, Lawrence S. "Of Bibliological Mendicancy," *College and Research Libraries,* 14:373-78 (Oct. 1953).

To Doctor R. Essays Here Collected and Published in Honor of the Seventieth Birthday of Dr. A. S. W. Rosenbach, July 22, 1946. Philadelphia: [Privately published], 1946.

West, Herbert Faulkner. *Modern Book Collecting for the Impecunious Amateur.* New York: Little, 1936.

Winterich, John Tracy. *Collector's Choice.* New York: Greenberg, [1928].

Wolf, Edwin, 2nd, with John F. Fleming. *Rosenbach: A Biography.* Cleveland: World, [1960].

Wroth, Lawrence Counselman. *The Chief End of Book Madness.* [n.p.,

1945?]. 15ₜ1₁p. Reprinted from the Library of Congress *Quarterly Journal of Current Acquisitions*, v.3, no.1, Oct. 1945.

MISCELLANEOUS REFERENCES ON RARE BOOK LIBRARIES

Adams, Randolph G. "Librarians as Enemies of Books," *Library Quarterly*, 7:317-31 (July 1937).
———— "Who Uses a Library of Rare Books?," *English Institute Annual, 1940*, p.144-63. New York: Columbia Univ. Pr., 1941.
American Library Association. Association of College and Research Libraries. University Libraries Section. *Rare Books in the University Library.* [Chicago, 1949].
Angle, Paul. "Reference Work in the Rare Book Room," in Pierce Butler, ed., *The Reference Function of the Library*, p.281-98. Chicago: Univ. of Chicago Pr., 1943.
Baughman, Roland O. "Selection and Acquisition of Rare Books and Related Materials at Columbia University," *Library Resources and Technical Services*, 2:271-78 (Fall 1958).
Bevis, L. Dorothy. "Rare Books in the College Library," *ALA Bulletin*, 53:149-52 (Feb. 1959).
Bishop, William Warner. "Rare Book Rooms in Libraries," *Library Quarterly*, 12:375-85 (July 1942).
Brewer, Frances J. "Special Problems of Special Collections," *College and Research Libraries*, 23:213-16, 255-56 (May 1962).
Burke, Redmond A., and Brewer, Frances J. "Place of Rare Books in the General Library," *Ontario Library Review*, 43:225-26 (Aug. 1959).
Carter, John. "Reflections on Rarity," *New Colophon*, 1:134-50 (April 1948).
Dougan, Robert O. "Some Thoughts of a Rare Book Librarian," *College and Research Libraries*, 19:388-94 (Sept. 1958).
Mixer, Charles Wilson. "Insurance Evaluation of a University Library's Collection," *College and Research Libraries*, 13:18-23, 29 (Jan. 1952).
———— "New Insurance for Library Collections," *Library Journal*, 79: 1539-43 (Sept. 15, 1954).
Nye, William J. "Trends in Rare Book Library Facilities," *College and Research Libraries*, 24:377-82 (Sept. 1963).
Purdy, George Flint. "Why Not Research in Rare Book Conservation?," *Library Journal*, 66:144 (Feb. 1941).
"Rare Books and Special Material in Museum Libraries: A Roundtable," *Special Libraries*, 52:9-21 (Jan. 1961).
Shaffer, Ellen. "Books with a Past, a Present and a Future—Rare Books," *Wilson Library Bulletin*, 34:138-44 (Oct. 1959).
Sharma, Jagdish Saran. "Place of Rare Books in a University Library," *Indiana Library Association Journal*, 13:16-18 (June 1958).

Silver, Rollo G. "Training of Rare Book Librarians," *Library Trends*, 9:446-52 (April 1961).

Smith, Harry Bache. "Gentlemen of the Old School," *The Colophon*, pt. 3, 1930. [8p.]

Snyder, Felix. "Rare Books and the Library Administrator," *Missouri Library Association Quarterly*, 10:6-10 (March 1958).

Van Arsdale, Jane Davis. "Rare Books Need Special Processing," *Library Journal*, 71:315-16 (March 1946).

Vosper, Robert G. "Rare Book Is a Rare Book," in University of Tennessee, *Library Lectures*, p.43-62. Knoxville: Univ. of Tennessee, 1955-57.

Wallace, Sarah Leslie, ed. *Friends of the Library: Organization and Activities*. Chicago: American Library Association, 1962.

Weidle, Catherine E. "Cataloging and Conservation of Rare Books," *Missouri Library Association Quarterly*, 19:14-18 (March 1958).